KU-257-100

Leading on Inclusion

Leading on Inclusion: Dilemmas, debates and new perspectives critically examines the current theory and legislative context of special educational needs and disability, and explores the enduring issues and opportunities that will affect future practice in all schools.

The central theme throughout the book asks the inevitable question 'What happens next?' and the expert team of contributors, drawn from a pool of teachers, academics and researchers, consider wide-ranging issues such as:

- the voice of young people
- whole school development and planning for inclusion
- educational change within the context of inclusion
- the pros and cons of multi-professional working
- inclusive and ethical research
- international perspectives on inclusion, SEN and disability
- the development of teacher education and the notion of 'joined up' thinking.

This forward-thinking and rigorously researched book will be essential reading for students, teachers undertaking school-based training, SENCOs, inclusion managers, higher education tutors and anyone with a professional interest in the future for inclusive education.

John Cornwall is Principal Lecturer in Special Educational Needs and Director for the Centre for Enabling Learning and Inclusion, Canterbury Christ Church University, UK.

Lynne Graham–Matheson is Principal Research Fellow in the Education Research Directorate, Canterbury Christ Church University, UK.

LIVERPOOL JMU LIBRARY

3 1111 01420 2228

Leading on Inclusion

Dilemmas, debates and
new perspectives

Edited by John Cornwall and
Lynne Graham-Matheson

 Routledge
Taylor & Francis Group

LONDON AND NEW YORK

First published 2012
by Routledge
2 Park Square, Milton Park, Abingdon, Oxon OX14 4RN

Simultaneously published in the USA and Canada
by Routledge
711 Third Avenue, New York, NY 10017

Routledge is an imprint of the Taylor & Francis Group, an informa business

© 2012 John Cornwall and Lynne Graham-Matheson

The right of the editors to be identified as the authors of the editorial material, and of the authors for their individual chapters, has been asserted in accordance with sections 77 and 78 of the Copyright, Designs and Patents Act 1988.

All rights reserved. No part of this book may be reprinted or reproduced or utilised in any form or by any electronic, mechanical, or other means, now known or hereafter invented, including photocopying and recording, or in any information storage or retrieval system, without permission in writing from the publishers.

Trademark notice: Product or corporate names may be trademarks or registered trademarks, and are used only for identification and explanation without intent to infringe.

British Library Cataloguing in Publication Data
A catalogue record for this book is available from the British Library

Library of Congress Cataloging in Publication Data
Leading on inclusion : dilemmas, debates and new perspectives / edited by John Cornwall and Lynne Graham-Matheson. -- 1st ed.
p. cm.
Includes bibliographical references and index.
1. Inclusive education--Great Britain. 2. Special education--Great
Britain. I. Cornwall, John, senior lecturer. II. Graham-Matheson, Lynne.
LC1203.G7L417 2012
371.9'046--dc23
2011026799

ISBN: 978-0-415-67621-2 (hbk)
ISBN: 978-0-415-67622-9 (pbk)
ISBN: 978-0-203-14400-8 (ebk)

Typeset in Bembo
by GreenGate Publishing Services, Tonbridge, Kent

MIX
Paper from
responsible sources
FSC® C004839
www.fsc.org

Printed and bound in Great Britain by
CPI Antony Rowe, Chippenham, Wiltshire

Contents

Acknowledgements

There are many people who have supported the work on the project and this book. The authors would particularly like to thank Phil Snell of the Department for Education, Micheline Mason, Emeritus Professor Janet Tod and Professor Brahm Norwich. Thanks are also due to many people who cannot be named – the teachers, advisers, headteachers, parents and pupils who were involved in the original project and from whom we have learned such a lot.

The contribution of the Training and Development Agency for Schools in funding the project is acknowledged.

Contributors

Mike Blamires is Principal Lecturer in the Faculty of Education at Canterbury Christ Church University. He was the Director of Content and Quality Assurance and Valorization for the Teacher Training Resource Bank (2004–2010) and also the deputy director of the Behaviour4Learning Initial Teacher Education Professional Resource Network (IPRN).

John Cornwall is Director of the Centre for Enabling Learning at Canterbury Christ Church University and has published widely on special needs, inclusion and the way education is managed. A former teacher and school Principal and Director of the four-year government project 'Strengthening Special Needs in Mainstream Schools', he is also a Research Psychologist and Educational Consultant with a national and international portfolio.

Alison Ekins works in the Centre for Enabling Learning at Canterbury Christ Church University (CCCU) delivering postgraduate courses to teachers and SENCOs in areas of inclusion, SEN and institutional development. She is also the Course Director of the new statutory training programme for SENCOs: National Award for SEN Coordination at CCCU.

Lynne Graham-Matheson is a Principal Research Fellow in the Education Research Directorate at Canterbury Christ Church University. Her research interests focus on professional development and special educational needs.

Peter Grimes is based at Canterbury Christ Church University, where he specialises in inclusive school development. Peter has worked as a consultant with Save the Children, Handicap International, UNESCO and UNICEF and supported the development of inclusive schools in south east Asia.

Fiona Hallett is a Reader in Education at Edge Hill University. **Graham Hallett** is a Senior Lecturer in SEN and Inclusion at the University of Cumbria. Fiona and Graham are joint editors of the British Journal of Special Education.

Anastasia Liasidou has been Senior Lecturer of Inclusive Practice and Education at Roehampton University, London and is currently an Assistant Professor of Inclusive Education at European University, Cyprus.

Bridget Middlemas is a Senior Lecturer in Special and Inclusive Education in the Department of Education at Roehampton University.

Gill Richards works at Nottingham Trent University in the School of Education as Director of Professional Development. She is involved with projects for student teachers, NQTs and SENCOs on inclusive practice and her research interests focus on 'learner voice' and inclusive education.

Sue Soan is a Principal Lecturer within the Centre for Enabling Learning at Canterbury Christ Church University. She has written a number of books on various aspects of additional educational needs, including the role of the SENCO, gifted and talented learners, looked after children and multi-agency working.

Cathy Svensson is the Subject Leader for Special and Inclusive Education in the Department of Education at Roehampton University.

David Thompson has worked within the higher education sector since 1998 in a variety of roles. He is currently Senior Lecturer at the School of Education, University of Wolverhampton where he teaches on the post-graduate special education needs and inclusion route.

Foreword

I am very pleased to provide a foreword for this new edited book about Leading on Inclusion. The book will have particular relevance in the new policy context established by the recent SEN Green Paper which, among other aims, aims to establish policy to correct what has been portrayed as a 'bias to inclusion' by the previous Labour Government. It is likely that the debates about inclusive education and inclusion in education will be revived by the Coalition's new policy stance. This is where this book will introduce a practice-based and evidence-informed overview of how to strengthen specialist support for pupils with special educational needs in mainstream schools and show how inclusion can be sustained.

There are various perspectives on what this supposed 'bias to inclusion' involves. One view is that inclusion is being presented as only about placement and not the other important aspects commonly associated with an inclusive commitment: participation, belonging and achievements. The progress and development made over the past decade or so have not, in this view, been recognised and celebrated. Another view has been that the Green Paper and Coalition Government policy is tilting against the previous government's commitment to international agency conventions and declarations, rather than recognising the realities of school practice and provision. The proportion of pupils in special schools has been shown by government statistics to have remained fairly stable and the small fall in special school numbers mainly reflects special school reorganisation. This book will inject a needed dose of reality rather than ideological rhetoric into debates about the field of special needs and inclusive education.

This book is an extension of a national project involving several universities to strengthen support for, and include, pupils with special needs. Its aim was to educate and develop specialist teachers who could work in an advisory capacity across mainstream schools. It arose from a Training and Development Agency (TDA) project to design a Masters qualification for teachers and advisers with experience of SEN and additional needs in their classrooms to lead on issues about SEN and inclusion in other settings.

The book sets this project in the wider policy context by examining how a commitment to social equality and opportunity can be achieved through the accreditation of professional development that supports inclusive developments. The editors have successfully brought together in this book the contributions of their collaborators, teachers and university researchers with experience of teacher education and training.

The book has a wide coverage and sets the 'leading on inclusion' theme in its rightful place as part of whole school planning and developments. The key orientation that emerges from these contributions is the importance of leadership, innovation, collaboration and problem solving. However, the constraints are identified as issues and tensions that need to be addressed in finding answers to the question of what is the way forward in the twenty-first century. Here is a book that will be very useful for teachers and senior managers in mainstream and specialist settings, support service professionals and those engaged in initial and continuing professional development.

Professor Brahm Norwich
Graduate School of Education, University of Exeter

Abbreviations

ACE	aids to communication in education
ASD	autistic spectrum disorder
BECTA	British Educational Communication Technology Association
BERA	British Educational Research Association
CAF	common assessment framework
CAMHS	Children and Adolescent Mental Health Services
CDC	Council for Disabled Children
CPD	continuing professional development
CSIE	Centre for Studies on Inclusive Education
CWDC	Children's Workforce Development Council
DCSF	Department for Children, Schools and Families
DES	Department of Education and Science
DfE	Department for Education
DfEE	Department for Education and Employment
DfES	Department for Education and Skills
DHSS	Department of Health and Social Security
DoH	Department of Health
DRC	Disability Rights Commission
FE	further education
ICT	information and communications technology
IQSA	Improving Quality Schools for All
IT	information technology
MEP	Micro Electronics Programme
NASUWT	National Association of Schoolmasters/Union of Women Teachers
NCET	National Council for Education Technology
NCSL	National College for School Leadership
NGO	non-government organisation
Ofsted	Office for Standards in Education
QCA	Qualifications and Curriculum Authority
SEMERC	Special Education Micro Electronic Resource Centre
SEN	special educational needs

SENCO	Special Educational Needs Co-ordinator
SENDA	Special Educational Needs and Disability Act (2001)
SENIT	Special Educational Needs and IT Group
SDP	school development plan
SIDA	Swedish International Development Agency
TDA	Training and Development Agency for Schools
UN	United Nations
UNESCO	United Nations Educational, Scientific and Cultural Organization
UNICEF	United Nations Children's Fund

Introduction

Leading on inclusion

Lynne Graham-Matheson

Background to the book

In 2004 the Training and Development Agency for Schools (TDA) invited tenders for a project *Strengthening specialist support for pupils with SEN and disabilities in mainstream schools* to design a Masters qualification in special educational needs (SEN). This was to be aimed at teachers and advisers with significant experience of SEN and additional needs in their classrooms, who were now being asked to lead on issues of SEN and inclusion in other settings. Canterbury Christ Church, in collaboration with four other universities – Edge Hill, Nottingham Trent, Roehampton and Wolverhampton – was successful in being awarded the project, and it is from the work on the project that this book emerged.

The project enabled the project team to gain a national perspective of current and intended future developments in the area of SEN and inclusion, including obtaining views from professionals in schools and services and from parents and carers of young people with special needs and disabilities. This book was inspired by this work as well as the objective of maintaining strong and well-argued positions around the need for socially just, equitable and supportive systems for all pupils, not just those with additional needs and disabilities.

The aim of the project – and this book – was to support specialist teachers (and others) who are increasingly working outside their own settings and in collaboration with other professionals: although they have experience as practitioners they may perhaps not have had the opportunity to look in any depth at the debates and perspectives which underpin SEN and inclusion. This book also provides a resource for others with an interest in SEN and inclusion because it looks at the 'bigger issues'. The change of government in the UK in 2010 heralded a change in approach towards inclusion and special needs, and at this time more than any other it is important to keep examining and re-affirming commitment to social equality and opportunity through education.

This book examines current theory and the legislative context of special educational needs and disability as well as the enduring issues and opportunities that will affect practice in twenty-first-century schools. Many aspects are considered, including the voice of young people, whole school development, educational change, ethical research, multi-professional working and international perspectives on inclusion, SEN and disability. The enhancement of the professional role of teachers as innovators, problem solvers and nurturing young lives is placed in the context of constraining ideas about curriculum in higher education and in schools. The central theme throughout the book asks the inevitable question 'What happens next?' Each chapter is written by well-informed and well-published teachers and researchers in higher education, all involved in teacher education and training. They look to the future and developments in professional training, higher education and national initiatives and opportunities in supporting twenty-first-century schools to provide good quality of life and learning for pupils with special educational needs and disabilities.

A key theme of the book is that issues around inclusion affect the whole school, and should be a matter of planning and development for the whole school, as an inclusive school leads to a better education for all children, not just those with SEN.

Leading on inclusion

Leading on inclusion is about leading change – helping teachers and schools to become more inclusive. Heifetz (1994: 15) suggests that the role of a leader is about helping people to tackle tough problems. It also means tackling new situations and looking at new ways of working, or as Fullan (2004: 2) says:

> Leadership is not mobilising others to solve problems we already know how to solve, but helping them to confront problems that have not yet been addressed successfully.

According to Fullan there are five components of leadership:

1 Moral purpose – acting with the intention of making a positive difference.
2 Understanding change – it is important to understand the *process* of change, for example:
   • the goal is not to innovate the most
   • it is not enough to have the best ideas
   • appreciate the early difficulties of trying something new
   • resistance needs to be turned into a potential positive force
   • a change of culture is the name of the game
   • complexity rather than a checklist.
3 Building relationships – if relationships improve, things get better.
4 Creating and sharing knowledge – turning information into knowledge is a shared process, and for that you need good relationships.

5   Making coherence – it is good to be at the edge of chaos because it is where creativity comes from, but effective leaders only tolerate enough ambiguity to keep the ideas flowing, but they seek coherence.

(based on Fullan 2004: 4)

These are all important factors for working effectively with others to promote change. Reporting on a case study of teachers of the deaf working with their mainstream colleagues, Lynas (2002) highlighted ways in which any specialist teacher might work to contribute to inclusive goals:

• teachers of the deaf *shared* their skills and knowledge – they did not keep their specialisms to themselves
• teachers of the deaf were *supportive* and *encouraging* to mainstream colleagues – they did not undermine them
• teachers of the deaf expected to *learn from their mainstream colleagues* and work with them to arrive at solutions to problems
• teachers of the deaf preferred to be perceived as *collaborators* rather than external consultants
• teachers of the deaf maintained a *proactive stance:* they did not simply complain when things were not right – *they made things happen*
• teachers of the deaf's primary goal for their pupil was *independence in learning* – they did not want their deaf pupils in the long term to 'need' them.

(in Farrell and Ainscow 2002: 160, original emphasis)

These factors show how teachers and advisers can take a leading role to bring about change, making schools more inclusive so that they benefit all children and young people. We hope that the chapters in this book will provide a framework for this work, by showing the dilemmas, debates and perspectives involved in thinking about inclusion.

A guide to the book

The book begins with an introduction to the history of inclusion and SEN, referring to key documents from the UK and internationally, such as the *Warnock Report* and the *Salamanca Statement*, through to the Coalition Government's Green Paper published in 2011. It also briefly considers the different models of disability.

Chapter 2 argues that children, particularly disabled children and those with SEN, need to be given a voice. It looks at the issue of pupil voice in school, particularly the role of school councils, and considers the issue of adults 'filtering' children's views. There is a focus on initiatives such as the *UN Convention on the Rights of the Child* and the DfES's *Working together: giving young people a say* and it raises a number of questions around how young people with SEN can be moved from the margins, including the issue of labelling. Lundy's

(2007) model for eliciting pupil voice is suggested as a way of enabling schools to listen to pupils, and the chapter concludes that the main 'cost' is time – time to create confidence and engage all learners.

Chapter 3 suggests that the quest for inclusion calls for a radical restructuring of traditional schooling in order to accommodate learner diversity in non-discriminatory and effective ways and changes need to go beyond bureaucratic and technical issues. Change is a multi-layered process that entails collaborative problem-solving procedures and collaborative practices and inclusive school leadership is important. The chapter focuses on the role of the special educational needs co-ordinator (SENCO), seeing SENCOs as an enforcer or 'lever' of change. It is noted that the SENCO role can take many forms, which may not always be compatible with a whole school approach to diversity, and argues for the SENCO role to be professionalised so that SENCOs can take leading roles in inclusive schools.

Chapter 4 acknowledges that issues around inclusion and SEN often focus on the day-to-day issues of the classroom, but suggests it is also important to look at wider influences that impact on inclusion and whole school development. The chapter highlights issues that can cause tension – such as the standards agenda and other policy pressures and what can be conflicting guidance. It describes the school development plan as a way of conceptualising school ethos and planning and moving towards whole school inclusion. School leadership and management must also be in tune with inclusion: teamwork and having committed teachers is also important. The chapter concludes that moving towards being an inclusive school can be a difficult and complex journey.

Chapter 5 considers school systems and processes, and argues that to be effective in meeting the needs of pupils with SEN they must be whole school systems, not just something that is 'done for pupils with SEN'. This represents a key shift in thinking, involving deeper consideration of the importance and impact of shared inclusive values and cultures in schools. Recent government policy and national strategies have meant an increasing focus on intervention for pupils who are underachieving, helping to embed the idea that such support is not just for pupils with SEN, but these interventions must be underpinned by a whole school commitment to inclusive values and principles. Inclusion should meet the needs of all pupils based on the principle of removing barriers to learning and participation (Booth and Ainscow 2002). Case studies show the importance of inclusive cultures in schools based on shared values and the individual processes involved in co-ordinating provision are seen as part of a dynamic model.

Chapter 6 examines inclusion from the perspective of classroom design. The beginning of the chapter has a brief summary of relevant policy documents, identifying how schools can develop inclusive classrooms, with a definition of an inclusive classroom and what needs to be considered in school design. It also describes listening to the student voice, staffing and teamwork, organising groups and classes and providing other spaces in school to support inclusive learning and teaching such as nurture groups. The chapter concludes that learners need to feel welcome in the classroom, and that best practice is not static but always evolving.

Chapter 7 provides a consideration of issues around multi-professional working, giving a historical overview going back to Bronfenbrenner (1970) and his view that children with SEN need an holistic approach with support from more than one agency or profession. The chapter suggests that, several years on from the implementation of policy to promote multi-professional working, in practice there are additional layers of bureaucracy with time consuming and administratively heavy practices, which have hindered the establishment of effective multi-professional relationships and changes in terminology have led to confusion and mistrust. Detailing the factors that lead to the success of multi-professional working or act as barriers, the chapter concludes that professionals working together can achieve positive outcomes for children but the 'one size fits all' approach will not always work: multi-professional working is not primarily about systems and processes but effective communication, the sharing of professional expertise and respect.

Chapter 8 traces the development of technology to support learners with SEN over the past 25 years or so. It highlights some of the issues encountered in the early days and notes that even though there was little formal research then it was clear that the computer could have dramatic effects for some children. Transfer and generalisation were important issues – could the achievements made from using a computer help progress away from the computer? Have children with SEN who make progress using a computer lost out from not mastering traditional skills alongside their peers? The chapter refers to an Ofsted (2002) report that found teachers did not know when and how to intervene in pupils' use of technology. It notes that the definition of e-learning given in *Towards a Unified e-Learning Strategy* (DfES 2003c) does not identify any criteria to evaluate learning with technology, suggesting this might be because technology has become such an important part of education/everyday life generally. Investment in interactive whiteboards has moved the focus from pupils to what the teacher can do with technology – technology has become taken for granted but its power to include learners has been overlooked.

Chapter 9 looks at issues around participatory and emancipatory research and acknowledges that moral and ethical dilemmas inherent in researching marginalised learners are complex and as relevant to teachers as they are to researchers, using Sockett's (1993) definition of the major virtues central to the moral character of teaching professionalism. Three case studies highlight some of the issues in research. The chapter concludes that educational leaders and those with responsibility for inclusion and SEN have a crucial role to play in empowering the voice and reflective capacity of all members of the school community: the necessary virtues should not be limited to classroom practice but should provide the basis for school-based research leading to school development characterised by emancipatory, empowering and ethical research-led practice.

Chapter 10 draws on a case study from Lao PDR to illustrate the development of more inclusive practices and systems in international contexts, focusing on the way teachers develop their understanding of inclusion. The chapter begins with a very brief description of education in Lao and then describes its inclusive education project that ran from 1993 to 2009. It discusses the concepts of inclusive and quality education and notes that the concepts of child-centred, child-friendly and active learning are beginning to permeate school development initiatives in Lao and elsewhere in south east Asia, linked to the development of UNICEF's child-friendly schools. The research showed the importance of working within a framework that responds to local culture and context and suggests that a long-term ethnographic approach is the only realistic way to work with schools in communities. The chapter concludes that cultural factors can be a barrier to change but are not always taken into account.

The final chapter draws together the preceding chapters and concludes with the thought that we need to move forward from our current education system, which is still based on Victorian values and ways of working, into one which is in accord with the technological, social, political and ethical changes which have occurred, and is more inclusive.

Chapter 1

How did we get here?

A brief history of inclusion and special educational needs

Lynne Graham-Matheson

Introduction

It is said that the past is a foreign country where they do things differently (Hartley 1953), and that is certainly true of inclusion and special educational needs (SEN). We have come a long way – though many would say not far enough – since the Egerton Commission pronounced in 1889 that

> The blind, deaf and dumb and the educable class of imbecile … if left uneducated, become not only a burden to themselves but a weighty burden on the state. It is in the interests of the state to educate them, so as to dry up, as far as possible, the minor streams which must ultimately swell to a great torrent of pauperism.
>
> (in Riddell 2002: 4)

In today's more enlightened times it is uncomfortable to note that the 1921 Education Act required local authorities to record the numbers of 'feeble-minded' and 'backward' children so that separate education could be provided.

In 2010 Hodkinson said that special education in England had been subject to rapid development over the past 25 years, particularly in relation to inclusion. He suggested that the 'current push for the implementation of inclusive education' could be an example of policy development and philosophical thought outpacing practice, so that the most vulnerable learners might be 'crushed by the weight of political policy, philosophical thought and ideological doctrine that seemingly dominate the current educational discourse' (Hodkinson 2010: 61).

Looking back at where we have come from helps to understand where we are now, so this chapter gives a very brief introduction to the background to inclusion and SEN – because in an education context inclusion is usually viewed in relation to SEN.

Early days

In the nineteenth century there were four levels of special condition – idiot, imbecile, feeble-minded and moral-defective. Idiots were seen as ineducable and excluded from the education system, imbeciles were placed in asylums and the others in special schools. Discourses on education at that time produced the medical and charitable models of disability. The medical model viewed children's development and behaviour in terms of internal biological differences, so that conditions were within-child defects or deficits and external factors such as poverty had no bearing on the disability. The charitable model saw disabled children as tragic figures to be pitied.

At the beginning of the twentieth century ideas were emerging that it was not just children with very evident disabilities – the blind and the deaf, for example – who needed special education, but any children who were 'different'. The legal context for integration and inclusive education in England and Wales began with the Education Act 1944, which stipulated that children with severe disabilities were to be educated in special schools wherever possible, although those with less serious disabilities could be educated in mainstream schools.

Special educational needs

The Committee of Enquiry chaired by Baroness Warnock in 1978 was a landmark, following the longest ever investigation into special education in England, Wales and Scotland. The Committee noted that the labelling of children requiring special education used negative terms – *educationally sub-normal* in England and in Scotland *mentally handicapped*. Even though the definition of special education in the Education (Scotland) Act 1969 had the merit of referring to children with emotional or behavioural difficulties as well as those with physical or intellectual disabilities, it was still negative:

> education by special methods appropriate to the requirements of pupils whose physical, intellectual, emotional or social development cannot, in the opinion of the education authority, be adequately promoted by ordinary methods of education.
>
> (DES 1978: p46)

The Warnock Committee said this definition ignores both the qualities and features which make special education 'special' and the fact that many children, at some time during their school career, need extra help. The Committee's research suggested that only two per cent of children needed separate, specialist education provision, with a further 18 per cent requiring special provision in mainstream schools. The Committee was the first to use the term *special educational needs*, which had the more positive effect of moving the emphasis to needs rather than within-child defects and deficits, saying we have adopted the concept of SPECIAL EDUCATIONAL NEED, seen not in terms of a particular disability, which a child may be judged to have, but in relation to everything about him, his abilities as well as his disabilities – indeed all the factors which have a bearing on his educational progress.

(DES 1978: 37)

In 2010 1.7 million children in the UK were identified as having special educational needs (DfE 2011a). The Education Act 1981 came out of the Warnock Report and required local authorities to provide suitable support and resources to meet needs identified in a statement of SEN. For the first time this imposed a duty on local authorities to ensure that children with SEN were educated in mainstream schools, so long as

- this was in accordance with their parents' wishes
- the child's SEN could be met in the mainstream school
- the education of other children in the school would not suffer
- the placement was compatible with the efficient use of resources.

(Hornby *et al.* 1995: 3)

According to Roaf and Bines (1989) the changes following the Warnock Report illustrated a shift in emphasis from medical or psychological criteria of assessment towards an 'educational, interactive and relative approach' (p. 6) taking into account all factors which have a bearing on educational progress. This social model of disability sees special needs not in individual or deficit terms but in relation to the requirements of curriculum and schooling, meaning that inappropriate teaching materials and techniques could be seen as having generated, or at least exacerbated, learning difficulties experienced by learners.

In contrast to the American system, which stresses disability, since Warnock the UK education system has tended to focus on need. Norwich (1996), for example, suggests children can have a range of different needs:

- *individual needs* arising from characteristics which are unique to the child and different from all others
- *exceptional needs* arising from characteristics shared by some children (e.g. visual impairment or high musical abilities)
- *common needs* arising from characteristics shared by all (e.g. the need to belong).

(original emphasis)

The tradition in the field of special education and the processes that relate to children identified as having SEN are rooted in identifying individual differences. Nind (2005) describes the two contrasting positions, characterised by Thomas and Loxley's conception of shared need:

> Children who are slow to learn – for whatever reason – need the same in order to learn as any other child … our humanity tells us they need interest, confidence, freedom from worry, a warm and patient teacher.
>
> (Thomas and Loxley 2001: 26)

and Aird's notion of difference:

> The needs of disabled children are radically different from those of the average child. These needs must be given proper status.
>
> (Aird 2001: 10)

The Warnock Committee's emphasis on need was intended to bring an end to the categorisation that had existed previously, but the idea of needs is still deficit based (Tomlinson 1982). In the event SEN became a label in itself, a way of categorising children as if they were a homogeneous group. As long ago as 1989 Pumfrey and Mittler wrote an article suggesting that 'the concept of SEN has now outgrown its usefulness and should be laid to rest', taken up again by Mittler (2000). It is also open to interpretation, so that what is defined as SEN (and thus requiring additional support) in one school or area is not so defined in another. A report by the Centre for Studies on Inclusive Education (CSIE) in 2005 found 'disturbing' local variation – pupils with statements of SEN in one local authority area were 24 times more likely to be placed in segregated education than those in another area.

Barton (1988) suggested that 'special needs' is a euphemism for school failure, while Richmond (1979) expresses concern over the use of the term 'special'. Richmond suggests there is nothing special about schools ensuring they are teaching effectively, that children are learning, that the curriculum is appropriate and there is a suitable environment with advice and support. This resonates with current debates around the existence of distinctive SEN pedagogy (in Ellis *et al.* 2008). Corbett (2001) also argues that inclusion means responding to individual needs, so the 'special' is redundant.

A focus on disability – however defined – also tends to obscure the difficulties children may experience through poverty or disadvantage, for example. Roaf and Bines (1989) argue that looking at rights and opportunities is better than a focus on need. In this they follow the American ideal with a strong emphasis on rights in education, emphasising civil rights, equity and dignity. Roaf and Bines say that a 'lack of dignity and respect is all too often associated with "having a need"' (2004: 21).

The *Salamanca Statement* (UNESCO 1994) went beyond SEN and was a catalyst for much of the education policy in the UK which supported more inclusive practices in schools:

> The guiding principle that informs this Framework is that schools should accommodate all children regardless of their physical, intellectual, social, emotional, linguistic or other conditions. This should include disabled

and gifted children, street and working children, children from remote or nomadic populations, children from linguistic, ethnic or cultural minorities and children from other disadvantages or marginalised areas or groups.

(UNESCO 1994: 6)

The *Statement*'s connection with the UN gives it an influential human rights context. This could be seen as problematic (for example, Low 1996) because the 'moral high ground' of the human rights approach could be said to have limited debate – inclusion is morally and socially right and thus incontestable. The stance taken by the Centre for Studies on Inclusive Education (CSIE), for example, is that all children have a right to an inclusive education. The notion of rights, though, is controversial. Others would argue, for example, that children in mainstream education have a right not to have their education disrupted by a child with behaviour problems.

The Disability Discrimination Act 1995 did not mention inclusion or access to education, leading to a major debate about the government's continuing tolerance of discrimination against disabled children and young people. It was not until 2001 that the Act was amended by the Special Educational Needs and Disability Act (SENDA) to cover every aspect of education (Ellis *et al.* 2008). The *Special Educational Needs Code of Practice* (DfES 2001a), which was revised from the *Code* published in 1994, emphasised a stronger right for children with SEN to be educated in a mainstream school. Also in 2001, *Inclusive Schooling* (DfES 2001b) provided statutory guidance including, 'Mainstream education cannot be refused on the grounds that the child's needs cannot be provided for within the mainstream sector' (p. 9). This placed a duty on schools to be able to accommodate every child (Tassoni 2003).

Hodkinson (2010) notes that the evolution of inclusive educational policy began with the election of New Labour in 1997. *Curriculum 2000* was founded on three inclusionary principles:

1 setting suitable learning challenges
2 responding to pupils' diverse learning needs
3 overcoming potential barriers to learning and assessment for individuals and groups of pupils.

Thus, inclusion was put firmly on the political agenda. Hodkinson argues, though, that the concept of inclusion refers only to children deemed to have SEN and their relationship with mainstream schools – the terminology of weakness and disability is patronising and degrading.

From integration to inclusion

Inclusion has changed in focus, moving on from notions of integration. Integration was concerned with including children with SEN in mainstream schools, having its origins in the early 1900s and welfare pioneers who believed in a non-segregated schooling system (Thomas *et al.* 1998). The Warnock Committee reported on and endorsed the three types of integration they had seen:

1   locational, where there were special units or classes in ordinary schools so little real integration took place
2   social, where children in a special unit would eat or play with mainstream peers
3   functional, where children would be in regular classes full or part time.

The Committee referred to integration – known as mainstreaming in the USA or normalisation in Scandinavia and Canada – as recognition of the *right of the handicapped to uninhibited participation in the activities of everyday life,* using the definition of the Snowdon Working Party:

> Integration for the disabled means a thousand things. It means the absence of segregation. It means social acceptance. It means being able to be treated like everybody else. It means the right to work, to go to cinemas, to enjoy outdoor sport, to have a family life and a social life and a love life, to contribute materially to the community, to have the usual choices of association, movement and activity, to go on holiday to the usual places, to be educated up to university level with one's unhandicapped peers, to travel without fuss on public transport ...
>
> (DES 1978: 99)

Although it is often thought that the Warnock Committee strongly promoted the idea of integration or inclusion, it did not. Its clear support for special schools is seen by some as at least partly to blame for the slow progress in integration and inclusion:

> For special schools the future holds both challenge and opportunity ... whilst there will probably be some decrease in the number of special schools, we see a secure future for them as the main providers of special education for severely and multiply handicapped children in increasingly close collaboration with ordinary schools.
>
> (DES 1978: 149)

So, children with learning difficulties or disabilities were to be integrated, or fitted, into mainstream schools but there was no expectation that all pupils with SEN would be functionally integrated. The strong inference was that the child would fit into the school, not that the school would be adjusted to accommodate the child (Mittler 2000). By the early 1990s serious reservations were being expressed about the value and practical operation of integration – integration was merely concerned with 'distributive calculus', or placing children in mainstream schools, not with the quality of their experience (Slee 1996).

'Inclusion' was first used in preference to integration or mainstreaming in July 1988, according to Thomas and Vaughan (2004). Concerned about the slow progress of integration in education, a group of Americans meeting in Toronto came up with the concept of inclusion, to better formally describe the process of placing children or adults with disabilities or learning difficulties in the mainstream. A radical change, the use of the word inclusion caught on quickly in Canada and the USA, but it was a few years before it was accepted in the UK and elsewhere.

Ainscow *et al.* (2006b) suggest that inclusion can be defined in two ways – a descriptive definition of inclusion reports on the variety of ways inclusion is used in practice, whereas a prescriptive definition indicates the way the concept is used. They developed a typology of six ways of thinking about inclusion:

- inclusion as a concern with disabled students and others categorised as 'having special educational needs'
- inclusion as a response to disciplinary exclusion
- inclusion in relation to all groups seen as being vulnerable to exclusion
- inclusion as developing the school for all
- inclusion as 'Education for All'
- inclusion as a principled approach to education and society.

(Ainscow *et al.* 2006b: 15)

Over the years in which he has been working in this field, Booth (1999) has moved from writing about integration to inclusion, following the conventions of the time, but has consistently rejected the use of the term 'special educational needs'. Writing in 1983, Booth argued that using 'integration' to mean bringing handicapped children into mainstream schools might imply that the necessity of involving children in the educational and social life of the school is finished once they are in the school building, and it might be seen to mean that handicapped children have a greater right to participation in ordinary schools than other children.

In the *Index to Inclusion* (2002), Booth and Ainscow refer to barriers to learning and participation rather than SEN, a term which they suggest has considerable limitations, including conferring a label that can lead to lowered expectations and may deflect attention away from the difficulties experienced by other learners without the label. In the *Index* inclusion is seen as an ideal, something for schools to aspire to and move towards. Inter alia, inclusion in education is defined as:

- valuing all students and staff equally
- increasing the participation of students in, and reducing their exclusion from, the cultures, curricula and communities of local schools

- restructuring the cultures, policies and practices in schools so that they respond to the diversity of students in the locality
- reducing barriers to learning and participation for all students not only those with impairments or those who are categorised as 'having special educational needs'
- recognising that inclusion in education is one aspect of inclusion in society.

There is no agreed definition of inclusion. Expressed in the simplest way, there are three viewpoints on inclusion as it relates to children with SEN:

1   Children with SEN should be educated in special schools which can best meet their needs.
2   Most children should be educated in mainstream schools but with some children in special schools which can meet the most severe needs.
3   All children should be educated in mainstream schools.

There is an underlying tension between the characteristics that all learners share and the characteristics that distinguish them (Nind 2005). Corbett notes that in the past there has been a view

> that inclusion meant bringing those outside ('the special') into the privi-
> lege of mainstream without acknowledging that many mainstream learners
> can feel excluded by a restricted curriculum, inflexible pedagogy and hier-
> archical ethos.
>
> (Corbett 2001: 1)

and argues that

> A responsive school climate, which views problems as challenges and not
> obstacles, is a key factor. The focus is on institutional systems, attitudes,
> flexibility and responsiveness rather than on the 'special needs' child. In
> order to provide such a highly developed level of inclusiveness, schools
> have to be willing to work consistently on improving and adapting their
> pedagogy. It has to be a pedagogy which relates to individual needs, insti-
> tutional resources and to community values: a connective pedagogy.
>
> (Corbett 2001: xiv)

Excellence for All Children: Meeting Special Educational Needs (DfEE 1997) expressed the government's commitment to the development of an inclusive system, setting out targets for 2002 which fell into six main areas:

- standards expected of children with SEN would be raised
- effective support and involvement of parents of children with SEN, including support of an independent 'named person'

- increased inclusion of children with SEN in mainstream schools
- emphasis on practical support rather than procedures
- more training and support for teachers and other education professionals, especially SENCOs
- effective partnership and information exchange between service providers, local authorities, social services and health authorities.

The earlier White Paper *Excellence in Schools* launched the New Labour Government's educational crusade (Armstrong 2005), placing educational policy in the school effectiveness and improvement agendas. According to Armstrong (2005) the language of individual pupil needs was rejected and replaced by a policy focused on the actions required to transform failing schools into successes and raise individual pupil achievement. This causes confusion, as the field of SEN focuses on individual need. The confusion is compounded by policy documents (DfES 2004a, 2005e) that consider the underachievement of pupils with SEN in the context of a *Code of Practice* that bases part of its definition of SEN on making inadequate progress.

Removing Barriers to Achievement points out that it is not the location (special or mainstream school) which is the main element in defining inclusion, as

> Inclusion is about much more than the type of school that children attend: it is about the quality of their experience and how they are helped to learn, achieve and participate fully in the life of the school.
>
> (DfES 2004a: 25)

It clearly also sees a role for special schools:

> special schools providing education for children with the most severe and complex needs and sharing their specialist skills and knowledge to support inclusion in mainstream schools.
>
> (DfES 2004a: 26)

This is ambiguous – the policy is for inclusion, but only up to a point. This is a concern for those arguing for full inclusion, but also those who wonder where the line is drawn:

> But what does inclusion mean in practice? Does it mean that the local school should provide for 100 per cent of the local pupils, for 99 or 98 per cent or some other proportion? Does it mean that all pupils should be educated together in the same class or the same school, and with the same teacher? Should particular schools include particular pupils, thus enabling pupils to attend mainstream though not their local school? Does it include on-site or off-site units?
>
> (Evans and Lunt 2002: 2)

LIVERPOOL JOHN MOORES UNIVERSITY
LEARNING SERVICES

In relation to schools and education, inclusion is a term which still causes much debate. For many people inclusion refers to all children and their rights and entitlement to education, but for others inclusion is still very much rooted in SEN. Ofsted defines inclusion as the process of educating children with SEN alongside their peers in mainstream schools (Ofsted 2003), but a focus on children who are seen as having SEN can ignore or marginalise the needs of other children, for example those from minority ethnic groups, those whose first language is not English or traveller children. The National Curriculum views inclusion as the creation of 'learning environments ... which respond to pupils' diverse needs' and provide opportunities 'for all pupils to achieve, including boys and girls, pupils with special educational needs, pupils with disabilities, pupils from all social and cultural backgrounds, pupils of different ethnic groups including travellers, refugees and asylum seekers, and those from diverse linguistic backgrounds' (DfEE/QCA 1999: 31).

Low (1996, in Croll and Moses 2000) highlights a central issue in current thinking about inclusion. At the theoretical level 'inclusion as an educational ideal has the "moral high ground", but at the day to day level of the thinking that informs educational policy its position is much less secure' (p. 2). As Croll and Moses point out, this is illustrated by the 1997 Green Paper *Excellence for all Children* (DfEE 1997) which fell into the familiar pattern 'of expressing strong support for the principle of inclusion while, at the same time, qualifying this support to the point where it is hard to see any particular policy direction being indicated' (p. 2). In the same paragraph, there is support both for inclusion and special schools:

> There are strong educational, as well as social and moral grounds for educating children with special educational needs with their peers. We aim to increase the level and quality of inclusion within mainstream schools, while protecting and enhancing specialist provision for those who need it.
>
> (DfEE 1997: 43)

In *Evaluating Educational Inclusion* (2000), Ofsted defined inclusion as being far broader than pupils with SEN:

> Educational inclusion is more than a concern about any one group of pupils such as those pupils who have been or are likely to be excluded from school. Its scope is broad. It is about equal opportunities for all pupils, whatever their age, gender, ethnicity, attainment and background. It pays particular attention to the provision made for the achievement of different groups of pupils within a school. Throughout this guidance, whenever we use the term different groups it could apply to any or all of the following:
>
> • girls and boys
> • minority ethnic and faith groups, travellers, asylum seekers and refugees

- pupils who need support to learn English as an additional language (EAL)
- pupils with special educational needs
- gifted and talented pupils
- children 'looked after' by the local authority
- other children, such as sick children, young carers, those children from families under stress, pregnant schoolgirls and teenage mothers, and
- any pupils who are at risk of disaffection and exclusion.

(Ofsted 2000: 4)

Inclusion in education cannot be considered in isolation as it sits within a political and societal context. Loxley and Thomas (2001) suggest that the notional commitment to inclusion in England and Wales at both national and local (school) level sits within a larger scenario 'which many would interpret as antithetical to inclusion' (p. 291), producing a central tension and inconsistencies. There is a particular problem in some schools caused by a policy to admit and work with any child, whatever their difficulties or level of ability, and the pressure to achieve results and do well in league tables.

Debates centre on addressing the credibility gap between the rhetoric and reality of inclusive education (Clark *et al.* 1998). Two consistently emerging areas for debate concern the 'right' and 'might' of inclusive education: the 'right' is centred around philosophical issues and the human rights agenda, with a belief that meeting individual children's needs overrides an ideological commitment to inclusion concerns (Croll and Moses 2000). The 'might' is politically led and tends to focus on the educational context, with a perceived tension between the development of inclusive practices and the continuation of national academic attainment targets. Governments have supported apparent paradoxes in policy and practice, including selective education based on academic ability for some, exclusion from mainstream education based on behaviour for others, the continued use of the term special educational needs and individual education plans and the option for parents to choose special school placement. While some contend that segregation and exclusion are socially constructed and thus can logically be deconstructed to promote full inclusion, others argue that this reasoning is flawed (Fuchs and Fuchs 1994; Zigmoid and Baker 1996).

Dyson argues that there is a fundamental contradiction within the UK education system between 'an intention to treat all learners as essentially the same and an equal and opposite intention to treat them as different' (2001: 25). A similar argument has been put forward by Rustemier (2002), who says that the aims and purposes of education in the UK are at odds with human rights concerns for inclusion and with education which should develop 'respect for human rights and fundamental freedoms' (p. 23). She quotes from the report of the UN Special Rapporteur following her visit to the UK in 1999:

> Emphasis on education-as-investment and on competitiveness tends to undermine education which is defined by the objective of strengthening

the ties which bind people … the impact of the league tables has been to penalise schools' investment in learners with disabilities and thus to hamper the adaptation of mainstream schools to children with disabilities, segregating them in special schools.

(Rustemier 2002: 23)

In 2005 Baroness Warnock made what was widely publicised as a 'u-turn' when she said that

There is increasing evidence that the ideal of inclusion, if this means that all but those with the most severe disabilities will be in mainstream schools, is not working.

(Warnock 2005: 32)

And so, inclusion should be rethought:

If it is too much to hope that it will be demoted from its present position at the top of the list of educational values, then at least let it be redefined so that it allows children to pursue the common goals of education in the environment within which they can best be taught and learn.

(Warnock 2005: 50)

Stating that 'Inclusion should mean being involved in a common enterprise of learning, rather than being necessarily under the same roof' (2005: 36), Warnock suggested that the government should consider the definition of inclusion suggested by the National Association of Head Teachers in 2003:

Inclusion is a process that maximises the entitlement of all pupils to a broad, relevant and stimulating curriculum, which is delivered in the environment that will have the greatest impact on their learning. All schools, whether special or mainstream, should reflect a culture in which the institution adapts to meet the needs of its pupils and is provided with the resources to enable this to happen … Inclusive schooling is essential to the development of an inclusive society. It involves having an education service that ensures that provision and funding is there to enable pupils to be educated in the most appropriate setting. This will be the one in which they can be most fully included in the life of their school community and which gives them a sense both of belonging and achieving.

(Warnock 2005: 1)

This change of heart just serves to illustrate that inclusion cannot work unless it is both driven and supported by policy and properly resourced. It does work effectively in countries such as Canada, where money that would be spent on expensive special schools is directed towards the mainstream.

Every Child Matters, published in 2003, followed the inquiry into the death of Victoria Climbié and made a commitment to reform children's services to prevent vulnerable children 'falling through the cracks between different services' (DfES 2003a: 5). Taking a more holistic view of the lives of children and young people, it identified five outcomes all children should achieve:

- being healthy
- staying safe
- enjoying and achieving
- making a positive contribution
- economic well-being.

(DfES 2003a: 6-7)

According to Cheminais (2005: 1), this represents

> a more legislative framework within the Children Act 2004 that works in synergy with other key government strategies to drive forward a holistic approach to learning and development.

In September 2010 Ofsted published a review of SEN and disability (Ofsted 2010a), commissioned to evaluate how well the legislative framework and arrangements served children and young people with SEN and/or disabilities. The review found both widespread weaknesses in the quality of what was provided for children with special educational needs and evidence that the way the system is currently designed contributes to these problems. The review team found that, despite extensive statutory guidance, the consistency of the identification of SEN varied widely, not only between different local areas but also within them and children and young people with similar needs were not being treated equitably and appropriately. Across education, health services and social care, assessments were different and the thresholds for securing additional support were at widely varying levels. The report recommends, inter alia, that evaluation should focus on outcomes for children and young people, not on whether they have received the services prescribed, and schools should stop identifying pupils as having SEN when they simply need better teaching and pastoral support. It calls for a review of the statutory framework for SEN, particularly the *Code of Practice*.

As this book was prepared for publication, the Coalition Government published its Green Paper *Support and Aspiration: A new approach to special educational needs and disability* (DfE 2011b). Among its proposals are simplification of the system and a reduction of bureaucracy, more control for parents over support for their child and family, a revised *Code of Practice* and tackling the 'problem of over-identification' in schools by having a single category for children whose needs exceed what is normally available in schools.

Of concern to many is the intention to remove what the Green Paper describes as the 'bias towards inclusion' – parents of children with statements of SEN will be able to express a preference for any state-funded school. The government will also 'prevent the unnecessary closure' of special schools, giving parents and community groups the power to take them over.

In a letter to the *Guardian* published on 12 March 2011, ten professors of special and inclusive education said that the Green Paper infers inclusion is a privilege to be earned, rather than a 'socially just and fair approach to schooling with benefits for all'. This, they suggest, means that for many this will mean their likely exclusion from mainstream schools and thus from the 'big society' the government intends to create. This was disputed in a response from Minister Sarah Teather (published 14 March) who emphasised the need for parental choice over schools for their children. But the Green Paper certainly appears to focus on needs and disabilities, thus turning the clock back to the medical model of disability, and away from a focus on inclusion.

Conclusion

In this chapter it has been possible to give only a very brief overview of the background to SEN and inclusion, mentioning some of the main developments and policy documents. It is a confusing picture, not least because there are no agreed definitions of 'special educational needs' or 'integration' or 'inclusion', and the interpretation of these terms can depend on the context in which they are used.

There are a number of dilemmas and contradictions. Trying to implement a philosophy of inclusion means a conflict with other features of the education system – competition, league tables, academic attainment, for example – so there is a rhetoric versus reality situation which comes down to issues of resourcing, teacher confidence and so on.

As education generally takes place in groups, the school system does not always see or appreciate learners as individuals. Robinson (2011 [2001]: 57) compares schools with factories and says that schools are based on principles of standardisation and conformity, with children moving through the system by age group, with all the five year olds together, all the six year olds together and so on 'as if the most important thing that children have in common is their date of manufacture'. Because of this, the concepts of inclusion and individuality can have an uneasy relationship – rather like adolescents who want to be different but at the same time need to belong. There must be a balance, but once policy and law become involved the balance becomes socially defined, thus there can be winners and others who do not fare so well.

One suggestion is that to test whether we need a policy we need to envisage a world without it – inclusion may be flawed, but without it as a philosophy we would be back where we were at the beginning of the twentieth century.

One thing we do know is that the only person the education inclusion agenda has real meaning for is the child or young person with additional needs who experiences it and needs to make sense of it. It is this group that, as a society, we should want to help and support, and yet even today it is still this group that we seek the least information from.

Chapter 2

Perspectives on special educational needs and inclusive practice

Whose views count?

Gill Richards

Introduction

What are 'special educational needs'? The simple answer takes us back to the Warnock Report (DES 1978) where special educational needs was a concept embedded within the report and subsequent legislation, policy and initiatives. Although government terminology has changed over time to include special needs and disabilities, disabled children, learning difficulties and disabilities, the young people to whom these labels referred have remained those originally identified by Warnock as experiencing a learning difficulty that required some form of special education.

The more complicated answer to this question draws on wider perspectives that challenge both the concept and such terminology. Hall (1997), for example, criticises the whole concept of 'special' educational needs and some disabled writers such as Rieser (2001) argue against the use of terminology that infers the 'difficulty' lies solely within the individual. Such opposing views lead to different notions of what type of education is appropriate for young people with these labels, creating confused expectations amongst families and professionals. Thus the power of labels and those bestowing them cannot be underestimated. Self-naming, determining what we are called, involves the very essence of power. When others select labels for us and impose them irrespective of our views, they serve to depersonalise us. It is then a simple move to make other decisions based upon the label, which in turn affects our wider experiences.

So, how do we know what young people are thinking? Giving young people a 'voice' sounds simple and straightforward! With the UN *Convention on the Rights of the Child* (1989) Article 12 assuring children's rights to express their views on matters affecting them, and subsequent government initiatives such as *Every Child Matters* (DfES 2003a) and the *2020 Vision* (DfES 2007b) reinforcing this, schools and other agencies have been encouraged to view the voice of children and young people as providing a positive contribution to evolving practice.

But is it that simple? Fundamental to having a voice is first being able to speak about what matters to you rather than responding to other people's priorities, and second, having what you say 'heard' and valued. In an education world where those with power exercise considerable control, children and young people often find that their views are considered secondary to those of adults, and in particular professionals and experts.

This chapter explores some of the complexities involved in listening to children and young people within the context of competing perspectives that include government, professionals, experts and parents. It starts by reviewing some of the more generic issues of schools listening to their learners, before focusing upon the deeper issues concerning the perspectives of children and young people identified as having special educational needs or being disabled.

Listening schools: engaging all or controlling the favoured few?

Most schools have developed a range of systems for listening to their learners. Typically these include school councils, questionnaires or surveys, focus groups, curriculum evaluation and consideration of new developments. While some of these make their pupils feel valued and active participants within their community, others may be less well developed, leaving pupils feeling on the periphery of decisions made about them. Even where there are apparently effective systems within schools, key questions still arise – can pupils make their perspectives heard on matters that *they* view as important and do they *all* feel able to contribute?

Some schools welcome pupil views on academic matters, even in reviewing teaching and being part of interviewing panels for new staff, whereas others see this as a step too far. Such concern was expressed by Chris Keates in her speech at the 2010 NASUWT's national teachers' union conference:

> The appointment of staff is a serious and important undertaking. It is important that the person eventually appointed to the job can be confident in their new role and is empowered to act with authority. The reality of involving pupils directly in the appointment process has the potential to place these considerations in jeopardy.

While this statement raises general issues for schools to consider, such as how pupils (or indeed, any member of an interview panel) is prepared for the role of interviewer and how they will later interact with an appointee, the implication here is that pupil participation should be limited to matters not perceived by staff to be 'serious and important'. This leaves us with a serious question: which matters are deemed appropriate by schools for pupils' engagement?

So, what are the experiences of pupils and how can schools learn about these? It could be argued that what we learn from pupils can rest simply on the methods we use and who we ask. However, even if we only focus on this, there are many tensions involved in accessing pupils' perspectives.

Osler (2010: 1) argues that, 'Although schools are designed for children and young people, they are rarely designed in co-operation or in partnership with students.' She identifies the problem to be staff believing that they know what pupils think and over-influenced by a vocal minority, with the result for many pupils being that 'their perspectives and consequently their needs, often remain invisible'. This vocal minority can be seen by their peers to be an 'elite group', as reported by Morrow in a Pupil Voice Conference (2006), where young people in her study expressed their frustrations when the 'favourites get picked and the rest get played as fools'. Osler noted similar frustrations in her own study, where young people stated:

> Give us a voice, not just some poxy little council which decides how much the price of chips are.

> Student councils are pointless and teachers don't actually respect and encourage our opinions, they try and force their own on us.
>
> (2010: 110)

Although these views may be particular to the school councils in the study, they do raise some fundamental questions about how this popular approach to seeking pupils' perspectives works in practice:

- Who decides the agenda? Do adult agendas routinely override those of pupils?
- How are members selected? Are they truly representative of their groups, or are some elected because they are more vocal, socially skilled, favoured or compliant?
- Do representatives really represent others' views and how are they prepared for this role?
- Who controls the conversations? Is everyone heard? Is the language used accessible to everyone?
- Is the ethos unthreatening so that pupils feel comfortable in giving honest views?
- How are records made of meetings? Are *all* views recorded unfiltered?

Decision making requires information. Morrow (2006) argues that this information needs to include an understanding of the 'rules of the game' within schools, so that pupils can grasp the wider picture and make decisions based on the knowledge of what may or may not be possible. This supports Osler's argument that pupils need a transparent process to enable them to understand how and what they can influence because 'ineffective or tokenistic school councils are more damaging to students than no council at all' (2010: 118).

Ineffective systems arise where pupil views are only sought on issues perceived by staff to be important and where feedback becomes a mechanistic chore to fulfil policy requirements. Compounding this can be inaccessible procedures that are difficult for individuals to understand and a lack of time to enable staff to genuinely listen. When this happens, schools appear to enter into consultation while still remaining firmly in control of the agenda (Richards 2010). In such circumstances, pupils are less likely to engage with the process or take it seriously, and can become quickly frustrated with reinforced feelings of disempowerment.

The issue of adults often being seen to know best is relevant here. Whilst staff clearly have professional expertise and responsibility for what happens within schools, pupil perspectives may differ from theirs on a range of matters, not least on what is perceived to be serious and important. Teachers may rightly believe that they know what is in the best interests of their pupils, but they can still learn a great deal from engaging with them on a wide range of topics. This does not infer that teachers should pass over decision making to pupils: pupils generally just want to have a say and be involved, but do want to be taken seriously. This, Cullingford suggests is problematic, arguing that, 'We have not yet learned to listen to their voices, let alone hear them. Perhaps we do not like the implications of what they are trying to say' (2005: 210).

Of course, different perspectives may conflict with each other and even reflect intolerant or anti-democratic views. Managing this successfully engages with the concept of 'community cohesion' where schools are expected to develop their learners' sense of belonging within a society that shares a common vision, values individual diversity and promotes tolerance (DCSF 2007a). There might not always be a 'neat' solution, but open discourse can increase understanding of alternative views – we can only test our achievement of cohesion if we know what others in our community think – it is easy to be tolerant if our 'knowledge' is built on assumptions!

It can be one thing to know young people's perspectives, but quite another to act upon them. Hearing what pupils say, without applying 'adult filters', can result in schools having to cope with completely unexpected requests or criticisms. This requires a confident and flexible staff group to be open to such feedback and manage uncomfortable decisions, but more positively, it can also offer innovative ideas from very different perspectives. Responding to pupils' views does not mean automatic agreement with all that they say: staff have a responsibility to consider the wider context and use their professional expertise when making judgements. What is important to many children and young people is that, having made their views known, they receive a response, preferably from someone with authority. Frustrations can arise when feedback seems to 'disappear' within decision-making structures and participants are left uninformed of any subsequent action, or when nobody 'important' engages with their ideas (Richards et al. 2007).

What about disabled young people?

The UN *Convention on the Rights of the Child* (1989) Article 12 made children more visible, moving their participation from marginal to central within schools (Rix *et al.* 2010), but there is still the question posed earlier in this chapter – are all young people able to participate or are some still positioned within the margins?

Many of schools' general concerns about whether children are mature enough or have the insight and competence to engage in decision making are compounded when considering those identified as having special educational needs or disabilities. It is not uncommon for them to suffer from what Rix *et al.* (2010: 118) describe as 'pervasive paternalism', where their capacity to participate is doubted or even considered impossible. Where there is a view that adults, and in particular parents, are best placed to take decisions on pupils' behalf, this is exacerbated for many children with special educational needs, who are often seen as in need of receiving professional advice rather than being capable of contributing to discussions about matters that affect them (Gwynn 2004; Mason 2005). Even the *UN Convention on the Rights of the Child* (1989) Article 12:1 assurances leave room for doubt with its reference to 'the child who is capable of forming his or her own views', and due weight 'being given in accordance with the age and maturity of the child'. While on one level this sounds eminently sensible, it opens up a world of interpretation around what *is* a child's 'capability' and 'maturity', and *who* decides?

Morris (1992: 10) argues that 'Our vision is of a society which recognises our rights and our value as equal citizens rather than merely treating us as the recipient of other people's good will.' Her view echoes earlier demands emanating from the civil rights movement and adopted by many disabled groups – 'Nothing about us without us' (Charlton 1998: 3). The context of rights is important because these provide entitlement to respect and dignity. If we deny anyone their rights we deprive them of their equal status with others. As Freeman (2010: 104) argues, many rights have not been freely bestowed, they were hard fought for, so must not be ignored or chipped away at because they are inconvenient: 'Without rights the excluded can make requests, they can beg or implore, they can be troublesome; they can rely on … others being charitable, generous, kind, co-operative or even intelligently foresighted. But, they cannot demand, for there is no entitlement.' This is often the case for pupils with special educational needs. They can be 'objects of concern' rather than learners in their own right, with their views represented rather than sought, known or understood; and in a world where children's rights are always trumped by parents' rights (Osler 2010), they can also be recipients of decisions resulting from their parents' rights being upheld rather than their own.

Recent government initiatives have demonstrated an increased commitment to listening to the views of children and young people with special educational needs or disabilities. The Department for Education and Skills' document *Working together: giving young people a say* (DfES 2004c) provided guidance for schools to help them increase consultation with all their pupils when making decisions. Ofsted's later review of special educational needs and disability (Ofsted 2010a) focused on the legislative framework, seeking to discover how successfully its arrangements had served children and young people. This provided a platform for a subsequent Ofsted inspector briefing (2011) where the importance of discovering learners' views was stressed, requiring them to discover how safe pupils with special educational needs and/or disabilities felt in school and to speak to vulnerable pupils and those frequently excluded about their experiences.

Focusing attention on this specific group of learners should certainly provide the basis for moving them from the 'margins' to a more centralised position with their peers. However, there are still questions to be considered:

- Whose views are sought, who do inspectors meet?
- How do pupils with very different needs represent each other?
- What happens if their views conflict with each other's views *and* with their parents' views?
- Are additional skills needed by inspectors to enable them to listen to learners who may have communication difficulties?
- If support is required for communication, how is confidentiality maintained and how might this intimidate learners?
- What happens to those who choose not to give their views? Is this respected?

Much of this mirrors the more generic issues raised earlier. Children and young people who are not used to having their views elicited may lack the advocacy skills or life experiences to articulate their opinions. They might not understand what is being asked of them or 'the rules of the game'. Who is selected to represent their peers can also involve particularly complex considerations, especially when individuals are expected to be the spokesperson for a wide range of disabled groups. The danger here is that disabled pupils' perspectives may be even more susceptible to becoming tokenistic. Divergent experiences from living with different special educational needs and impairments may become diluted through limited representation, and a pervasive view that professionals know best about their needs can serve to devalue their views further.

Contested labels: contested experiences?

There is a strong lobby from disabled activists which challenges the historical power that non-disabled people have acquired over their lives. Early impact of this power was apparent in the way that disabled people were treated by eugenicists in the nineteenth century, falling prey to policies of sterilisation and segregation within asylums and workhouses. Disabled people were seen as 'defective' and incapable of managing their affairs, necessitating medical professionals and other experts to decide how their needs should be met. The legacy of this, Mason (2011) and Rieser (2011) argue, still affects the lives of many disabled people today.

Labelling is still a key issue. Governments select and create legislation around their preferred labels for disabled children and adults, expecting others to adopt these. Charities utilise labels and images to encourage fund raising. Criticisms of this are often ignored or dismissed as misunderstanding, despite these coming from people directly affected. Public challenges have been mounted, often with limited success. For example, the international *Label jars not people* campaign by People First – an advocacy group representing disabled people – has had limited success with UK charities (Birklen *et al.* 1977). Mencap (derived from Mental Handicap), while claiming to be the 'voice of people with learning disability' (Mencap 2011), has continued to publically dismiss requests to change its name, despite acknowledging that many of the people it supports find this offensive (Durham 1992).

The label of 'special educational needs' is one that also engenders much debate. Hall's (1997) seminal discourse on 'Special Land', where pupils with special educational needs are often consigned after being rejected from mainstream activities, underlines some of the difficulties of this label. His reflections on the words 'special' and 'needs' draw attention to the complexities of the concepts hidden within these, arguing that 'special', with its connotations of something usually desired by society, changes within this context, becoming a euphemism for 'problem' within schools. Similarly, 'needs' implies *neediness* rather than a learning *requirement* that schools must provide and infers that the problem is located within the child and so requires remediation focused on him/her, rather than based on wider contextual issues such as teaching, learning and resources.

Many other writers raise similar concerns (Thomas and Vaughan 2004; Mason 2005; Ainscow 2007; Wearmouth 2009; Frederickson and Cline 2009; Richards 2010), arguing that labels can affect the way that teachers and others view and respond to pupils. The impact of this is clear: if one group of learners is seen as 'special' and therefore different from 'ordinary' pupils, then *ordinary* teachers may perceive teaching them as outside their capacity or requiring something additional from them. All of this can serve to reinforce 'an uncritical acceptance that *special* children need to go to *special* places for a *special* education' (Richards 2010: 91, original emphasis).

Concerns about the creation and imposition of labels are not new. Becker's 'Labelling Theory' (1963) argued that those with institutional power to impose labels on people can have a radical impact on their lives. He suggested that those who label others should consider how the person labelled might be affected, particularly where associated stereotyping and stigma could undermine their acceptance in society. This can be seen through language heard in schools today where pupils are referred to as 'the SENs' and 'the wheelchairs', and where pupils refer to themselves as 'special' without realising the wider implications for the way that society treats them.

It is often suggested by teachers and parents that a label is required to ensure that appropriate support and resources are identified and funded (Lauchlan and Boyle 2007; Loreman *et al.* 2010), but there is evidence that the situation is more complex. The Audit Commission (2002: 14–17) described the statutory assessment process that identifies pupils' special educational needs as 'a costly, bureaucratic and unresponsive process … which may add little value in help-ing meet a child's needs'. Similarly, Ofsted (2006) argued that the statutory assessments did not ensure quality of provision, and the British Psychological Society (2005) suggested that a statement of special educational needs created a barrier to inclusive practice through over-dependency on specialist resources. More recently, Ofsted (2010b: 5) criticised the mislabelling of special educa-tional needs, arguing that many pupils had been wrongly diagnosed: 'They were underachieving simply because the schools' mainstream teaching provi-sion was not good enough', concluding that 'relatively expensive additional provision is being used to make up for poor day-to-day teaching and pastoral support'. They also stated that their inspectors had found poor evaluation in schools of the quality of support provided, with the focus being on whether or not it was provided rather than whether it was effective.

So, to return to issues raised in the introduction of this chapter, labels are powerful, and when others select and impose them it can affect a pupil's wider life experiences. Expressing views about this is just one issue on which disabled writers voice their concerns. Inclusive education practice has become a highly contested concept with opposing advocates creating a battleground of opinions. Different experiences have led to impassioned appeals for more special schools, more inclusive practice and more mainstream support. Politicians, education professionals and parents all have a view, but where is the perspective of the child and disabled people who have actually experienced such education? Who acquires the greatest public platform and dominates the discourse?

An example of this was seen in 2005 when Baroness Warnock claimed to have changed her mind about inclusive education, arguing that it was unworkable for many young people with more complex needs. Supported by a number of vocal politicians and parents, Warnock commanded a significant public presence on television and in the national press. Dissenting views from disabled groups, other parents and educational professionals found access to a national public forum problematic, resulting in them needing to purchase an entire page of advertising space in the *Times Educational Supplement* (8 July 2005) to express their opposition to her views. More recently, when the gov-ernment sought views on developments for pupils with special educational needs for their Green Paper (DfE 2011b), the Alliance for Inclusive Education and other disabled people were offered the opportunity to engage with this, but their voices were few among many with contrasting perspectives.

The impact of whose voice dominates the public forum can be far reaching within schools. With increasing demands on teachers' time, many receive the plethora of government documents and popular teachers' press items with little opportunity to seek alternative perspectives on the issues raised. So, while they might be provided with (often summarised) reports and directives, they do not engage with the wider debate on these and remain unaware of other perspectives on matters such as the *2020 Campaign* (to end segregated education), endorsed by many disabled people's organisations including the Alliance for Inclusive Education, The British Council for Disabled People, People First and Disability Awareness in Action (Alliance for Inclusive Education 2005). These groups *of* disabled people may differ in their views from others professing to speak on behalf of disabled people who also tend to have easier access to public forums in which to present their views.

The context of teacher training within this debate is important for, as Murphy (1996) asserted, attitudes established during this time are difficult to change later. Whose voices do trainee teachers hear? How does their training prepare them to listen to *all* learners? The training curriculum should offer trainees an opportunity to learn from the experiences of disabled people directly, otherwise the impact may be twofold. First, they will not have access to the unfiltered views of disabled people, and second, this could lead to the impression that it is acceptable practice to hear some pupils' views second hand. Even the textbooks used on their courses have importance for they convey more than information; they convey values, attitudes and beliefs through their use of language, focus on particular aspects and omission of others. If tutors only promote the reading of government literature and academic texts, rather than materials produced by disabled people, this perpetuates the view that expert knowledge about disability is gained from professionals rather than those with direct experience. Engagement with disabled people is also important. Mason (2000) argues that experiencing disabled people as peers, equals and teachers has the greatest impact on individuals' attitudes, so a positive experience during training could have a far-reaching impact throughout teachers' careers.

What works? What can we learn?

Lundy's (2007: 110) model for eliciting pupil 'voice' contained four key elements:

1   space – children must be given the opportunity to express their views
2   voice – children must be facilitated to express their views
3   audience – the view must be listened to
4   influence – the view must be acted upon, as appropriate.

Following this model should enable any school to listen to any pupil, although vigilance may be needed to avoid the pitfalls identified earlier in this chapter.

Utilising these elements has provided the platform for several studies and reports of young peoples' experiences, producing a rich source of information for education professionals and parents. For example, *Count me in FE* (Anderson *et al.* 2003) offers insight into young people's views of their education:

People around me make the decisions – lecturers, parents, friends.

(p. 17)

Inside the class non-disabled people are fine, but outside they don't want to know.

(p. 21)

Most tutors are patient with me, but not all tutors have an awareness. I'm not a person who complains. I don't want to be a nuisance – it might annoy the tutors.

(p. 28)

Other reports demonstrate the different priorities of pupils. For example, Darby and Fairley's study (2002: 7–8) identified a potential conflict between pupil and teachers: 'Every time you finish like a page of work they come up and … then draw a smiley face and ruin your book. Don't do this.' Ofsted's report (2010a: 2) described what young people wanted for the future: successful relationships and friendships; independence, including the choice about who they lived with; choice about what to do in their spare time; and the opportunity to work. They also found that pupils' views on success differed from those of their parents (Ofsted 2010b). Pupils wanted to have relationships and friendships, choice about who they lived with, choice about what they did in their spare time and the opportunity to work. This contrasted with their parents who prioritised happiness, safety, access to work or purposeful activity and improvement in communication and basic skills. Determining the success or otherwise of inclusive practice also demonstrates the different priorities of those involved. Schools, driven by government targets, usually measure educational achievement, but pupils and disabled people regularly identify social inclusion and relationships as of equal importance (Mason 2005; MacKeith 2010).

Self-image was recognised by inspectors as a strong contributor to young people's engagement in learning and having a voice in matters that concerned them: 'In the best practice observed, young people had been well taught to make decisions from an early age, were given increasing responsibility as they grew up and were fully involved in making decisions that affected them' (Ofsted 2010a: 70). Rix *et al.* (2010) had similar findings to Ofsted, with young people emphasising the importance of friendships at school and expressing less concern about matters that worried their parents. They also discovered that the experience of high-quality relationships which were responsive to their feelings and views enhanced young people's participation.

All of this indicates that young people do have opinions and these may differ from those of others close to their daily lives. What is needed more than anything is their confidence in expressing a view that will be listened to and given the time to do it. Without this, strategies to engage them are unlikely to be successful. Young people with the most complex learning difficulties need this even more as they are most likely to be excluded from commonly used strategies. They are susceptible to having their views identified through 'observation' by professionals. The potential dangers of this are clear: a distinction is necessary between what is *defined* as pupils' views and what is *interpreted* as either their view or what is in their best interests. In the same way that earlier pitfalls to pupils' engagement were described, staff can encourage confidence in any strategy used by ensuring that pupils' 'voice' is respected and unfiltered by adults around them.

Conclusions

A key question relating to all of the issues raised in this chapter is, 'How do we see the role of learners in contributing to education discourse?' In particular, what role do we see for disabled people and children labelled as having special educational needs and disabilities? Accepting that they have a valuable contribution to make, not only on matters that affect them, but also on wider education matters affecting us all, requires us to consider who we listen to, how and about what? We must be prepared to be flexible and open to change, otherwise there is no point in listening. Adopting this approach can create a very different balance around decision making, moving us from relying on intuition and assumption to what MacIntyre (2010: 82) describes as 'collaborative, explicit and evidence-based decision-making'. Significant amounts are spent on information-recording systems within education – how much is spent on listening to learners? The main 'cost' is time, to create confidence and engage *all* learners. If we wish to move towards more inclusive practice, finding time is an excellent place to start.

Chapter 3

Theorizing educational change within the context of inclusion

Anastasia Liasidou and Cathy Svensson

Introduction

In recent years legislation has embodied an ongoing commitment to inclusion and given credence to the notion that pupils with special educational needs will be provided for in mainstream education (DfES 2001b). Such a commitment represents a robust philosophical stance in government, local authority and school level policy in recent years (Hallett *et al.* 2007). The introduction of the *Disability Discrimination Act* (DfES 1995) followed by *The Code of Practice on the Identification and Assessment of Special Educational Needs* (DfES 2001a) and *Special Educational Needs and Disability Act* (HMSO 2001) have each in their own way contributed to the paradigm shift initiated in the wake of the *Warnock Report* (DES 1978) which made provision for pupils with special educational needs to be educated in a mainstream setting. The publication of *Inclusive Schooling: Children with Special Educational Needs* (DfES 2001b) and *Removing Barriers to Achievement* (DfES 2004a) clearly set out 'the government's vision for the education of children with SEN and disability' and the provision 'of clear national leadership' (DfES 2004a: 9) in achieving that goal.

Now, in the twenty-first century, the right to inclusive provision for pupils with disability is an ethical assumption and failure by schools and colleges to amend discriminatory policy and practice is not only undesirable but unlawful. A consequence of developments over the past thirty years is that special schools are viewed as less favourable placements for pupils with disability. Some would go so far as to question the very right of segregated settings to exist and purport that their existence is an obstacle to human rights (Mittler 2000; Barton 1996). The message emerging from the literature and policy documentation reinforces the notion that mainstream schools appear to be synonymous with inclusive provision and by default, therefore, segregated provision and the notion of 'segregated but equal' is associated with discriminatory practice (Roaf and Bines 2004).

The quest for inclusion calls for a radical restructuring of traditional schooling so as to accommodate learner diversity in non-discriminatory and effective ways. Proponents of inclusive education are also proponents of radical school reform (Slee 2006; Ainscow 2005a) in order to promote sustainable school development (Sindelar *et al.* 2006). Norwich (2010: 86) places some of the problems, dilemmas and potentials pertaining to inclusive education within the remit of a general, and subsequently transformed, educational system. This said, legislative mandates promoting the realization of an inclusive discourse should also be concerned with promoting radical educational change and strategic school development in terms of teaching and learning. Changes should go beyond bureaucratic and technical issues (Riehl 2000), and embrace the ethical and critical dimension of the attempts to foster greater inclusive policies and practices (Lingard and Mills 2007; Ryan 2006a; Allan 2005).

The process of change is a multi-layered and demanding one that entails collective problem-solving procedures and collaborative practices (Kugelmas 2003) with a view to minimizing barriers to participation and enhancing achievement for all children in inclusive educational settings. Educational change necessitates a critical engagement with an assemblage of micro and macro dynamics perpetuating and sustaining a number of special educational imperatives, disguised under the banner of inclusion (Slee 1996). Top-down policy reforms geared towards the realization of an inclusive discourse are amiss unless complemented by attempts to cultivate new kinds of professional knowledge and practice predicated on the principles of an inclusive education reform agenda.

Deficit oriented approaches to dealing with disability and special educational needs should be challenged and substituted by whole school approaches intended to destabilize the special educational status quo. The individual gaze and the paraphernalia of its normalizing practices, aimed at singling out presumed defective individuals, have been superseded by an institutional gaze aimed at initiating educational change and promoting sustainable school development (Ekins and Grimes 2009; Fullan 2006). Towards this end, the emphasis should be directed to the need to initiate and sustain a process of radical school reform (Sindelar *et al.* 2006), which should be strategically managed and led by competent and well-informed agents of change within schools.

Inclusive school leadership is inexorably linked to the success of inclusion (Edmunds and Macmillan 2010; Rayner 2009; Kugelmas 2003). Principal leadership has been identified as a pivotal factor in promoting inclusive education and impacting the process of educational change towards this end (Theocharis and Causton-Theocharis 2008; DiPaola and Walter-Thomas 2003; Riehl 2000). The notion of leadership, however, is not solely embodied in the role of headteachers, but extends to include diverse forms of distributed leadership (Harris and Spillane 2008; Harris 2008; NCSL 2004). Huberman and Miles (1984) have paid prominent attention to the role of teacher leaders, who can become the 'enforcers' of the process of change (quoted in Sindelar *et al.* 2006: 318).

Within the UK context, SENCOs (Special Educational Needs Co-ordinators) have been increasingly seen as the 'enforcers' who are expected to lead a whole school process of development and change with a view to better responding to the needs of children designated as having special educational needs and/

or disabilities in inclusive mainstream settings (MacKenzie 2007; Cole 2005; Layton 2005). Lorenz (2002) discusses the changing role of SENCOs within the context of inclusion in order to facilitate organizational and ideological restructuring of current schooling.

This chapter will consider some parameters of the process of change within the context of inclusion by exploring the changing role of SENCOs in promoting sustainable inclusive school reform. Within this process, the chapter intends to explore dilemmas, paradoxes, current debates and new perspectives on the role of SENCOs as 'enforcers' and leaders of inclusive school reform. As Cole (2005: 304) suggests: 'If the SENCO is to act as an agent of change bringing inclusion into the mainstream discourse of school improvement, then the role needs to be closely interrogated now.'

Inclusive leadership and leadership for inclusion

Ryan (2006b) defines inclusive leadership as a form of leadership that promotes a particular aim: that of inclusive education concerned with identifying and transforming multiple and diverse forms of exclusion endemic to current schooling. The leadership role of SENCOs has been acknowledged as being of fundamental importance in enforcing a strategic development of schools (House of Commons Education and Skills Select Committee 2006; DfES 2004a; DfES 2001b).

Depending on the roles they are expected to embody, SENCOs can become the main 'enforcers' of transformative change. However, even though it has been long pointed out that SENCOs should be members of the senior management team, this recommendation is contingent on the discretion of headteachers and governing bodies (Pearson 2010; Wedell 2009). Without being institutionally empowered to play a leading role on inclusion, the SENCO's role is significantly limited to and subsumed within bureaucratic and standardized SEN management duties, as well as reactive approaches to providing learning support (Pearson 2010). Such practices are complicit in the maintenance of the status quo and undermine the process of transformative change.

The SENCO's role is confounded by the bureaucratic nature of current SEN provision that deflects attention from the more fundamental aspects of an inclusive education reform agenda in terms of teaching and learning (Pearson 2010; Szwed 2007a,b). It is currently reported that SENCOs have been increasingly overwhelmed by the 'audit culture' that stifles their potential to undertake a leadership role in developments pertaining to inclusion (Pearson 2010; Szwed 2007a,b). Dominant accountability regimes have precipitated a raft of performance indicators, which have acted, according to Ainscow (2005a: 119) as a 'double-edge sword', because while ostensibly they might be viewed as safeguarding accountability and transparency, the use of data can, in practice: conceal more than they reveal; invite mis-interpretation; and, worse of all, have a perverse effect on the behaviour of professionals. This has led the current 'audit culture' to be described as a 'tyranny of transparency'.

(Ainscow 2005a: 119–120)

It has been well documented that the bureaucracy of SEN has undermined the capacity of SENCOs to concentrate on issues of strategic school development and institutional reform within the context of inclusion (Pearson 2010).

It remains to be seen whether the requirements placed on governing bodies by the House of Commons Merits of Statutory Instruments Committee (2009) intended to ensure that new SENCOs undertake nationally approved training to obtain the National Award for Special Educational Needs Co-ordination – will enhance SENCOs' professional profile and niche in terms of undertaking a leading role in inclusive school reforms. Possibilities for change involve, among other things, fostering the development of SENCOs in order to become what Fullan (2006: 121) calls 'system thinkers in action' capable of thinking in 'bigger terms' and acting 'in ways that affect larger parts of the system as a whole'. This perspective is significantly reflected in the five outcomes outlined in the nationally approved training for new-to-post SENCOs, namely

- professional context
- strategic development of SEN policy and procedures
- co-ordinating provision
- leading, developing and supporting colleagues
- working in partnership with pupils, families and other professionals.

Levers of sustainable school reform and SENCOs as agents of changes

This section considers some of the 'levers' of change (Ainscow 2005a) that can promote sustainable inclusive school reforms. The notion of sustainability is an integral part of the attempts to initiate educational change, and is directly linked to the complex nature of inclusive education that should be regarded as a process rather than an end (Booth and Ainscow 2002). The notion of sustainability entails building 'the capacity of a system to engage in the complexities of continuous improvement consistent with deep values of human purpose' (Fullan 2005: ix). Cheminais (2010: 25) characterizes SENCOs as 'strategic leaders' who 'challenge complacency and relentlessly pursue the continual drive for further improvement'.

A crucial 'lever' for transformative change is 'to develop the capacity of those within schools to reveal and challenge deeply entrenched deficit views of "difference"'(Ainscow 2005a: 117). MacLean (2008) writes about the ethical dimensions of educational practice and the necessity for educators to explicitly examine the ways in which they adhere to arbitrary fabrications of normalcy, thereby sustaining and reproducing disabling assumptions and discourses. It is thus suggested that

> The realization of unwitting complicity in sustaining the hegemonic social structures that construct disablement of others is pivotal to creating the possibility for agency and change as discovery develops confidence and capacity for effective action.
>
> (MacLean 2008: 606)

In terms of the role of SENCOs and their contribution to the process of change, Pearson (2010: 32) writes that the role of the SENCO is

> grounded in a philosophical position and a set of values. How diversity is viewed and the existence of shared values and beliefs have consistently been linked to the successful development of inclusive practices.

Inclusive education is embedded in a complex web of philosophical positions and values – what Norwich (2010: 93) calls 'a plural values framework', whereby contradictory existing and emerging educational, social and political values are constantly juxtaposed, struggled over, contested and negotiated. The policy-making processes pertaining to inclusion can currently be characterized as a 'discursive battlefield', whereby differing discourses vie for ascendancy (Fulcher 1999; Ball 1993), thereby confounding policy constitution, dissemination and implementation. On the one hand, globalization promotes the ideologies of the market (Barton and Armstrong 2007), on the other hand, concerns for human rights, social justice and equality of opportunity (Rioux 2002: Barton 1993), along with a pronounced emphasis on the well-being and all-round development of individuals, feature strongly in policy documents (DCSF 2007b; DfES 2003b).

Not surprisingly, inclusion has been reported to be a prodigious challenge for all school leaders (McLaughlin 2009), including SENCOs, whose role is confounded by contradictory policy landscapes that foreground both 'inclusion' and 'excellence' (the latter solely measured against standardized achievement tests and consequent school league table positionings), something that creates tensions for schools in attempting to converge two inherently different agendas. Schools have been increasingly rendered accountable to meet certain 'standards' gauged against mono-dimensional and arbitrary 'fabrications' of successful schools (Ball 2004). These observations have certain ramifications in relation to SENCOs' professional standing and autonomy in order to promote inclusion.

Inclusion is occasionally used as a euphemism of exclusion (Barton 1988), which is rhetorically disguised within inclusive education policies. The latter are occasionally characterized by reductionism, in the sense that inclusion is constricted to the traditional special educational framework (Slee 2001), thus reflecting an obscure, ambiguous and essentially unchanged philosophical orientation. The uncritical adoption of hybrid discourses of inclusion gives rise to and consolidates a contradictory inclusive education policy landscape. As a result, educational practitioners experience 'confusion, frustration, guilt and exhaustion' (Allan 2008: 9) in their attempts to foster greater inclusive practices.

The proliferation of mono-dimensional versions of school effectiveness aligned with the standards agenda have given rise to neoliberal constructions of inclusion (Roulstone and Prideaux 2008; Armstrong 2005; Dyson 2005), whose overriding aim is to provide effective learning opportunities irrespective of educational placement. At a policy level, segregated placements are presented as being part of the inclusion agenda in terms of learning and learner participation (Lloyd 2008; Dyson 2005), while more recent policy initiatives go so far as to stipulate the necessity to 'remove the bias towards inclusion' (DfE 2011b).

While few would argue against the moral imperative that is driving the inclusion agenda, its links with rights, discrimination and equity ensure its continued advocacy. Nevertheless we cannot overlook or fail to challenge the quality of the implementation of that ideology and the multiplicity of practices endorsed in the name of inclusion. For this reason we question whether the default ratification of the ideology of inclusion in mainstream schools has inadvertently obscured the realization of that vision.

Given the above considerations, SENCOs' role can take many configurations within current schooling. Their role is not always compatible with a whole school approach to dealing with learner diversity. Emanualeson (2001) (cited in Pearson 2010: 32) distinguishes two kinds of enactments in terms of SENCOs' role, 'namely reactive (i.e. linked to a categorical approach to pupils' needs) and proactive support (i.e. adopting an interactive perspective).' Whilst the latter perspective is more aligned to the agenda of inclusive educational reform, the former stance necessitates a 'professionalization of the role of the SENCO' (Cole 2005: 304) in order to provide specialized teaching and compensatory measures of support for certain groups of children. It is questionable, however, whether the professionalization of the SENCOs' role can contribute to an inclusive reform agenda (Pearson 2010; Cole 2005; Layton 2005). As Cole (2005: 302) writes: 'How difficult is it for the SENCO to take on the role of agent of change for children still categorized as "special" and therefore "different"?' This tension can be better extrapolated in relation to planning and devising support for pupils on the autistic spectrum.

Historically, autism is embedded in the traditions of the psycho-medical paradigm linked to SEN (Kenworthy and Whittaker 2000; Hall 1997) and, as such, it embodies the contentions between the psycho-medical and the social political models of disability. The medical categorization of the disorder, its biological basis and the psychological theories which inform this are firmly embedded in a deficit model of need supported by the medical categorization of the disorder. Its strong genetic basis and gender biases in favour of males to the ratio of 4:1 are widely documented (Frith and Happé 1994). As a condition it can occur across the full range of intellectual ability. It is understood to represent extreme functioning in communication, imagination and socialization (Wing 1996) which interfere with notions of typical functioning and development. The 'social model of inclusion' from which understandings of inclusion are derived, on the other hand, lies at the other end of the continuum. Its affiliation to inclusion means it is embedded within the domain of social constructionist or creationist understandings of the world and contingent on this it embodies the rights discourse. The divergent influences, values and beliefs inherent in autism, by way of its affiliation to SEN and inclusion, go some way to explaining the tensions inherent in the role of SENCOs.

The question, therefore, is can these divergent positions be brought together in an inclusive setting, and if so, how? What is the role of SENCOs in merging these different methodological stances? SENCOs should reconcile these divergent viewpoints and dilemmas and align the perspectives of various stakeholders (local authorities, teachers, parents, children) under the light of fears for parental litigation and legislative anti-discrimination mandates with regard to disability and special educational needs (Cole 2005).

The notion of the 'professionalization' of SENCOs is susceptible to multiple understanding and enactments and it can potentially acquire new meaning in the current context of inter-agency collaboration, parental involvement and inclusive education (Pearson 2010). SENCOs' professionalizm can be redefined in terms of their capacity to act as key workers or lead professionals in bringing together support and information from diverse stakeholders with a view to providing more effective support programmes for certain groups of students in mainstream classrooms.

Cole (2005: 288) argues about the need for 'reprofessionalization' of this group of teachers so they become 'powerful and reflective practitioners who could be in a position to take on the mantle of inclusion within mainstream schools'. The aim should be to enable SENCOs to (re)conceptualize their role as being/becoming agents of change and identifying both possibilities and challenges towards this end. SENCOs' commitment to the process of change should be reinforced by national policy intended to address some of the problems and tensions endemic to their current role.

According to Fullan (2006) the process of change is undermined when there is no consensual approach to a shared vision. Similarly, inclusion demands a whole school approach to a culture and ethos that is embedded in shared values and principles (Booth and Ainscow 2002). The SENCO has the potential to play a lead role in the realization of that vision. No longer is the SENCO alone responsible for the identification, assessment planning and teaching of all children with SEN. The National Curriculum inclusion statement (DfEE/QCA 1999) clearly sets out the statutory duty of all teachers to meet the needs of all their pupils, and in so doing paves the way for a reconceptualization of the SENCO role. The previous government's strategy for inclusion, *Removing Barriers to Achievement* (DfES 2004a), underlines this vision with an expectation that the SENCO plays a key role in the management of change and more widely in the co-ordination of provision and the development of school policy. Nevertheless, the strategic vision as outlined in the strategy falls short of offering any specification on how that leadership role would be implemented. The following extract outlines the vision for the SENCO role as one that is

> a pivotal role, co-ordinating provision across the school and linking class and subject teachers with special educational needs specialists to improve the quality of teaching and learning ...

> (DfES 2004a: 58)

Furthermore it stipulates:

> We want schools to see the SENCO as a key member of the senior leadership team, able to influence the development of policies for whole school improvement.

> (ibid.)

The vision outlined is both operational and strategic and is further captured in the conceptualization of the SENCO role within the National Award for SEN Co-ordination (TDA 2009). Here, there is a clear expectation that the SENCO will work strategically to ensure the development of an inclusive school ethos and culture which removes barriers to learning and enhances educational opportunity and participation for all pupils.

This task however is not easy; it is fraught with challenges and assumes a re-professionalization of the SENCO role as strategic leader, facilitator, counsellor, enabler, expert and collaborator in leading strategic policy and practice while concurrently developing a whole school response to meeting individual needs.

The following case studies outline two different models of the SENCO role. Case Study 1 exemplifies the micro rather than macro dynamics and possibilities of the SENCO role in perpetuating and sustaining special educational needs imperatives. Simultaneously, it captures the bureaucratic and standardized SEN management duties contingent with reactive approaches to providing learning support (Pearson 2010). In this way, the maintenance of notions of normalcy and SEN provision dominates practice.

Case Study 1

In this primary school (School A), the SENCO role was offered to a teacher new-to-post as a professional development activity. The teacher had completed her induction year one year previously. As it happens, her specialist subject area was music. The school offered the new-to-post SENCO some training in the form of shadowing the outgoing SENCO for two weeks prior to her retirement. During this handover period, the new-to-post SENCO was introduced to the raft of documentation associated with the role and the key multi-agency personnel involved in provision.

In addition to taking on the SENCO role, the new-to-post SENCO taught a Year 3 class for four days a week with one day dedicated to fulfilling her SENCO duties. The new-to-post SENCO was extremely conscientious: she worked hard to understand the needs of the pupils on the SEN register, to meet parents, the teachers and teaching assistants and to set up individual education plans for those pupils identified as being on the Action Plus Register within the school. Setting up the multi-professional review for five statemented pupils proved onerous, nevertheless she played a key role in managing that process, in liaising with outside agencies and parents and in drawing together the necessary evidence from teachers and teaching assistants to develop a comprehensive profile of individual pupils' needs.

The time involved in the review of the statemented pupils was onerous and yet she was very aware of her statutory and professional duties in carrying this out. She completed a classroom observation of a pupil during a literacy lesson and considered this important evidence of the pupil's ongoing disengagement in his learning. She would present this alongside other varied evidence at the pupil's review meeting.

The new-to-post SENCO's days were filled by managing the process of writing targets, setting up intervention groups and collating information to justify the support offered to individual pupils, either on a 1:1 basis or within a group. In this way, the SENCO fulfilled her duties as outlined in the *Code of Practice* (2001), but her potential for driving the inclusion agenda was compromised because of the micro and bureaucratic nature of her tasks and her status as a newly qualified teacher.

The SENCO in Case Study 2 adopts a proactive strategic management role. She plays a key role in collective problem solving with staff and is intent on cultivating new kinds of professional knowledge and involvement in enhancing provision beyond those designated SEN. She adopts a whole school approach to inclusion which offers a framework of provision well beyond that aimed at singling out individuals. Instead, her role as a member of the senior leadership team embodies a strategic management role which facilitates both organizational and ideological restructuring in 'ways that affect the larger parts of the system as a whole' (Fullan 2006; 121) and over the longer term promotes sustainable school development.

Case Study 2

The SENCO in School B has nine years' experience as a classroom teacher. To date she has taught in two primary mainstream schools in very diverse settings, both in areas of severe social deprivation. She has also spent one year teaching in a special school for pupils with moderate learning difficulties. The school's policy is to ensure that, where possible, SENCOs teach in reception class as here they will get to know all the pupils at school entry and meet the parents and carers as they drop off young children at school. In so doing, they will have an opportunity to form an early and lasting relationship with them.

As a class teacher the SENCO has teaching duties in class for two and a half days and fulfils her SENCO role during the other half of the week. Her two and half days' time is ring-fenced by the governors in order to ensure the weight and importance assigned to her role and the need for consistency in managing change is recognised. This means that the SENCO is not called to cover staff absences at the last minute. Her routine of setting up and monitoring classroom support, completing observations, meeting parents, teachers, teaching assistants and multi-agencies is well established. More generally, she has been instrumental in putting in place a range of assessments for teachers and teaching assistants to use as a means of tracking pupils' progress against their predicted attainment and national curriculum levels. She views rigorous assessment as contingent on meeting personalized learning needs for all pupils and has championed this cause of the notion of assessment for inclusion for some years now. As a result, staff tracking of individual pupils is sensitive yet robust and informs personalized learning. The SENCO uses this to inform target setting and provision mapping across the school, which in turn feeds into school development planning. All staff have a very clear understanding of their role in assessment and monitoring all pupils and how this information feeds into school development planning. It is against this rigorous assessment framework that provision for individual needs is decided. In this way, teaching and learning activity is predicated on the principles of this wider inclusion agenda.

As a member of the senior leadership team the SENCO attends governors' meetings and supports the headteacher in making decisions about prioritizing funding to support SEN provision, in the light of the information she has collated on pupil progress. Following professional development offered through the new-to-post SENCO training, she has extended the remit of her role as a strategic leader in her own primary school to one that champions consultative and collaborative provision in neighbouring cluster schools, both mainstream and special schools. Here, she challenges staff to reconsider SEN provision linked with notions of normalcy to one that extends beyond the narrow framework of SEN provision and creates the capacity for effective action and the successful development of inclusive practice. Here, too, she promotes the role of assessment in enhancing inclusive provision and the sharing of good practice and staff expertise and resources across mainstream and special school settings.

Conclusion

The model of SEN provision as outlined in Case Study 1 has little currency within the wider discourse of inclusion. Instead it undermines any potential for transformative change and maintains a model of SEN provision linked with notions of 'normalcy' which fail to contribute to the inclusion reform agenda. This approach, according to Slee (2004: 63) remains 'a case-by-case approach in catering for special needs … in unchanging schools' and does not 'reflect epistemic changes where people frame disablement as the interplay of unequal power relations'.

Case Study 2, however, embraces a much more robust and strategic SENCO role capable of having an overview of strategic developments in school. In this case study, the SENCO has become the 'enforcer' of transformative change. Her role is pivotal in challenging complacency and in driving whole school improvement and the inclusive reform agenda. As a member of the leadership team she is exposed to strategic wider school development. Her management role is important to that end. Her strategic vision is not bound within the narrow confines of SEN provision but is set within a wider inclusive agenda. Interestingly, too, she does not view SEN and inclusive provision as being at odds with one another but two sides of the same coin, intended to enhance schools' responsibility to meet students' diverse needs. However, the notion of 'needs' is framed against the necessity to build schools' capacity to provide personalized learning and minimize barriers to achievement. The notion of 'assessment' plays a crucial role in this process insofar as it is not used as a way to 'match resources to student deficits in order that they do not disrupt the institutional equilibrium' (Slee 2004: 63). Rigorous assessment can constitute 'a potent lever for change' and can be 'seen as the life-blood of continuous improvement' (Ainscow 2005a: 119) when it is strategically used in order to track students' progress in terms of 'value added' performance criteria, measure the effectiveness of evidence-based strategies and interventions, review current policies and practices and plan the way forward (Mitchell 2008; Ainscow 2005a).

The SENCO's role should be reconceptualized, reframed and enacted against a systemic approach to devising, monitoring and co-ordinating provision for children designated as having SEN and/or disabilities. This approach deflects attention from individual pathology perspectives and concentrates on developing inclusive practices. SENCOs should be empowered not only to understand this context, but also to take the lead in initiating and sustaining changes towards this end.

Chapter 4

Whole school development, inclusion and special educational needs

Acknowledging wider debates

David Thompson

Introduction

When considering issues of school inclusion and special educational needs (SEN), it is very tempting – and quite understandable – to concentrate on classroom themes such as pedagogy, differentiating the curriculum, attending to specific needs and impairments, specific interventions, assessment and so on. In other words, the pragmatic day-to-day challenges that teachers face when attempting to implement inclusionary practice within the classroom environment.

This chapter asks you to think beyond the boundaries of the classroom and consider some of the wider influences that impact on inclusion and whole school development. Such an approach is moulded by processes, policies, politics, structures and personalities. Examples of a whole school approach to inclusion can take into account many factors, including the role of the governors, the management and leadership style of the school, the school ethos, the role of the school development plan (SDP), staff development, the impact of stakeholders such as parents and children, and external factors such as specialist organizations that support the health and well-being of the child. At a theoretical or policy level, the tension between the inclusion agenda and the standards debate also has a significant influence. In addition, evidence suggests that much more needs to be done to close the gap between school policy and practice in the classroom (Ekins and Grimes 2009: 10). Inclusion, and the ability to implement inclusive practices within the classroom, is inextricably linked with these external influences. Practitioners who are looking to lead on inclusion need to consider the conditions in place that manipulate (intentionally or otherwise) progress on inclusion and view their ambitions and achievements within this context.

One can, of course, learn from others in the process of developing and sustaining inclusion. For example, some argue for the need to 'look outside a narrow field of enquiry' when discussing school improvement strategy. 'There is much to be gained in the development of educational thinking by going beyond one's front door, and '"taking cuttings" from other people's gardens'

(Clough and Corbett 2006: 26). This chapter should act as a reminder to the reader to think eclectically in their quest for inclusion and whole school development. In terms of inclusion, disability and SEN 'promoting [disability] equality is a whole school approach and not a matter for a particular class or teacher ... [for it to be successful it must be] fully supported by the leadership team and embraced by the whole school community' (Sakellariadis quoted in Hallett and Hallett 2010: 25).

Competing agendas?

It is how one balances the commitment to inclusion with all the other pressures influencing a mainstream school that is problematic. That is not to say that being or trying to become an inclusive school (whatever that means exactly) is antithetical to other aspects of school development, but the evidence suggests that the path towards cementing such an aspiration is somewhat winding, with many diversions that compete for attention. The 'standards agenda' is clearly one such example where 'policy pressures' have to be negotiated (Ainscow *et al.* 2006a) whilst concurrently attempting to lead on inclusion.

The UK has witnessed a series of policy statements and legislation on the subject of inclusion and/or SEN (for example, the Special Educational Needs and Disability Act 2001, the *Every Child Matters* agenda, the *Lamb Inquiry* 2009), and internationally the UNESCO *Salamanca Statement* of 1994 is regularly cited. Yet these are counterbalanced by other policy pressures. Future direction and policy are subject to very different ideologies in the UK today as the agenda of the Conservative and Liberal Democrat Coalition Government begins to take root. No doubt such an ebb and flow away from and towards neoliberal agendas will be repeatedly enacted in other democratic countries and policy on inclusion will follow suit. Nevertheless, governments are pursuing a parallel and potentially more powerful policy – the standards agenda. This revolves around performance league tables, pushing up levels of attainment, standard assessment tests (SATS) and, ultimately, the drive to improve national skills levels and competitiveness in a global society (Ainscow *et al.* 2006b: 296). To what extent inclusion and standards are compatible is a moot point.

In principle at least, the standards agenda is 'entirely compatible with inclusive school and educational system development' but 'has concentrated on a narrow view of attainment' (i.e. literacy and numeracy) (Ainscow *et al.* 2006a: 296). 'The need for a plural, tolerant, inclusive education system sometimes sits uneasily with policy that foregrounds the benefits of choice, selection and the comparison of schools on the basis of their pupils' attainment.' The layers of policy are essentially incompatible: 'one conflicts with another' (Thomas and Loxley 2007: 107). The emphasis on individualism and the free market reflect the politics of the 'new right', whilst the stress on community and 'stakeholder welfare' reflect the 'new centre left'. This can leave schools somewhat beached; pushed and pulled by the tide of paradoxical policies.

A more radical and explicit interpretation argues that the 'rationing' of education has led to an 'educational triage' and an A–C economy whereby schools channel their efforts into students who have the potential to reach these grades 'such that higher-grade passes have become the supreme driving force for policy and practice at the school level' (Gillborn and Youdell 2000: 198). Further, that governments merely pay 'lip service' to 'equity issues' and that 'dominant approaches to the policy and practice of education actively reproduce and extend existing inequalities of opportunity' (Gillborn and Youdell 2000: 220). In 2010 the UK government announced that if less than 35 per cent of pupils in a school achieve the top A–C category then the school will be deemed as underperforming. This is an increase from the 30 per cent set by the previous government, so the pressure to jump to the attention of the standards agenda will no doubt increase. Whilst Gillborn and Youdell speak predominantly of race and class, it is not unreasonable to transpose this into disability and inclusion more generally. Such a bleak and sullied exposition of our school system suggests little room for manoeuvre when attempting to bring inclusion to the fore. However, this does depend upon the management and leadership, vision and ethos of the school, the direction it wants to take and how inclusion is 'mediated'. In addition, a discourse based upon the rights of the child may also help to counter the market-led approach to choice and standards and the silo mentality towards special educational needs – a term increasingly criticized for its growing use in a pejorative sense (Runswick-Cole and Hodge 2009).

Guidance can be confusing, however. Since 1999, Ofsted's inspection framework has also taken into account 'educational inclusion'. Their 2004 report on inclusion observed that progress has been made following the implementation of the 'inclusion framework', but they were also forced to conclude that 'a high proportion of the schools visited in this survey have still a long way to go to match the provision and the outcomes of the best. They are generally not reaching out to take pupils with more complex needs, especially if their behaviour is hard to manage' (Ofsted 2004: 23). The confusion generated by the reality gap between policy and practice and the 'mixed messages' that are transmitted is encapsulated by many authors (see Clough and Corbett 2006: 151–154; Ainscow et al. 2006b). Despite the apparent dichotomy of inclusion or standards, the relationship between standards and inclusion agendas as they intersect in schools is not the sort of simple opposition that some studies might lead us to expect. Agendas are mediated by the norms and values of the communities of practice within schools; they form a dialogue whose outcomes can be more rather than less inclusive (Ainscow et al. 2006b: 305).

The standards and inclusion agendas do not necessarily have to cancel each other out; progress can be made on both fronts within a school. Two of the questions asked include:

- Which aspects of supportive and collaborative practice help to make an inclusive school one that is also an effective school?

- Should a commitment to inclusive education necessitate a re-evaluation of priorities within the existing mainstream curriculum?

(Clough and Corbett 2006: 159–160)

Clearly, there are tensions between the two policy areas, or doubts as to how one can articulate them, and these can be transmitted into the delivery of school policy. The priorities in any development plan a school is constructing are potentially compromised between the need for improvement in league tables and progress towards whole school inclusion. Such compromise is influenced by internal and external factors; the latter often relating to societal and political pressures. Policy exists 'as part of a broad range of local and national debate articulated by the public, by professionals and by politicians about the nature of the society we live in' (Thomas and Loxley 2007: 94). Where does this leave us? Perhaps, in the first instance, practitioners such as SENCOs and other leaders who have a vested interest or ideological commitment to inclusion need to reassess documents such the school's SDP and consider:

- To what extent is inclusion strategy incorporated, compared to other demands and pressures?
- To what extent are aspects of inclusion prioritised within the SDP?
- How does the SDP set out the facilitation of inclusionary practice, and what measures are in place to support this process and record improvement?

(Ainscow *et al.* 2006b: 296)

We return to the SDP and leading on inclusion periodically throughout this chapter. In the meantime, these bullet points may help practitioners contextualize the school's current position on inclusion in the light of other priorities.

Planning for inclusion?

Probably the most consistent way in which the school ethos and planning is conceptualized is the SDP and it is this document that can sometimes reveal to what extent the school is geared towards inclusion. Generically, school development planning has been described as:

primarily a working document for use by the school. It will be based on the school's analysis of current levels of performance, its assessment of how current trends and future factors may impact on the school and set out priorities and targets for improvement for the period ahead.

(Department of Education, Northern Ireland 2005: 1)

The SDP is a by-product of the UK Conservative Government's 1988 Education Reform Act. This placed more autonomy and financial control in the hands of the individual school, at the expense of the local education authorities. Thus the SDP was identified as a way of accounting for these new responsibilities and managing funding in a systematic fashion. The SDP coincided with the introduction of the National Curriculum and therefore, in some schools, the plan began largely as a curriculum development plan but gradually took on a wider brief, while for others it included staff development and financial management plans.

The 'central tenet of school improvement is that the responsibility for change must lie in the hands of the school itself' (Stoll and Fink quoted in Mortimore and Whitty 2000: 12). A way of setting out change over a period of time can be articulated in a comprehensive SDP that has whole school inclusion as a core value. Such a document reflects the school ethos and is acted upon with vision and leadership, and this leadership is communicated through a distributed set of responsibilities and communities of practice. In other words, inclusion is not a 'silo' that is placed with one team or the SENCO. SDPs vary in size and detail for each school, and so too does the emphasis on inclusion within each plan. School development planning is a vehicle by which change is generated, the SDP characterizes the way that a school sees itself and its further development and improvement. But if the SDP is seen as a vehicle for change and improvement, then any move towards an inclusive culture must be seen within the context of, and integral to, whole school development. Inclusion should be defined clearly as part of the core values of the school and incorporating the whole school community. Overlapping definitions of inclusion also provide us with a framework from which to build upon and flesh out strategies for whole school inclusion. These include:

- Reducing barriers to learning and participation for all students.
- Increasing the capacity* of schools to respond to the diversity of students … in ways that that treat them all as of equal value.
- The putting of inclusive values into action in education and society.

(Ainscow *et al.* 2006b: 297)

*As an important adjunct to this, I would suggest the training and enabling of professionals to develop communities of practice that support inclusion.

Further, the SDP process will involve:

- The confirmation of the school's ethos, culture and aims.
- An assessment of the school's current position, its strengths, areas for improving the quality of learning and teaching and the various factors which will influence the management and development of the school over the next three years.
- The anticipated level of resources and its management.
- What the school wants to achieve within a defined number of years, in most cases expressed in terms of quantifiable targets for future performance.

- How it intends to bring about these achievements.
- When, and how, it will measure progress.

(Department of Education, Northern Ireland 2005: 1)

It is clear from these six contingencies that the aims for inclusion and how it might be planned, delivered and measured could be encapsulated in each bullet point. If progress is to be made towards whole school inclusion, then such a process must be applied to the SDP as a way of complementing the standards agenda with a clear articulation of the school's inclusion policy. In practical terms the SDP might be articulated through self-evaluation, data collection and analysis, provision mapping, target setting and developing inclusive interventions (Ekins and Grimes 2009).

Leading on inclusion requires evidence of progress, and fundamental questions need answering. These include which aspects of support and collaboration aid inclusion? Is a re-evaluation of priorities necessary? And what training and professional development is needed to help facilitate and enable progress on inclusion? Answering these questions (and this is not an exhaustive list by any means) may provide stepping stones towards whole school inclusion. Evidence of good practice and what already works well within the school allows the celebration of success and potentially provides the building blocks for further development. Developing the SDP and the role of inclusion may infer that this will automatically contribute to the effectiveness of the school. However, we should be cautious about the research and the data we derive from evidence on effectiveness, and indeed how we measure or decide on what is effective, and for whom? The discourse on effectiveness is problematic. Careful consideration is warranted before we assume that improvement will automatically mean that those more marginalized are incorporated into notional gains with respect to improvement and how inclusion is measurably achieved (Slee *et al.* 2005). Using accurate data effectively to help identify and support those who are vulnerable or underachieving is an important tool for developing an understanding of inclusion matters in a school and supporting 'inclusion in action' (Ekins and Grimes 2009). Leaders on inclusion will need to think very carefully regarding whether the school can genuinely claim to be achieving and continually improving on inclusion; data analysis will help them do this (Franks in Hallett and Hallett 2010).

The conclusion that 'The idea that more inclusive approaches can emerge out of internal school dynamics and that it is possible to intervene in these dynamics opens up new possibilities for national policy' (Ainscow *et al.* 2006a: 306) forces us to consider exactly what are the 'dynamics' in school and how one can 'intervene'. One way of doing so is through a whole school inclusion policy that is embedded in the SDP, forming a significant part of the self-evaluation process. This must be underpinned through developing communities of practice and 'transformational' leadership and management.

Leadership

Guidelines and plans must be applied more specifically to inclusion policy within the school if progress is to be made. For this to happen, it requires school leadership and management that is ideologically in tune with inclusion and inclusive practice as a core principle, if not a raison d'être. One can see that, from some of the following common features highlighted by numerous authors, elements of an inclusive school culture include a strong emphasis on leadership and management:

- staff who subscribe to a set of values that are key to inclusion
- leaders committed to those values
- leadership that distributes responsibilities for inclusion
- governors and parents who are supportive of inclusive practice.

A concept of leadership applied to a school context incorporates 'School leaders, understanding and accommodating the contexts in which they operate, mobilize and work with others to articulate and achieve shared intentions to enhance learning and the lives of learners' (Dempster 2009: 22). Such an approach could easily encompass the whole school inclusion process.

For inclusion to be fully embraced by the school, clearly it needs to form a significant part of the management team's agenda. Leadership is an important factor in both school improvement and in the move to become a more inclusive school. Headteacher, staff and the governing body all need to show enthusiasm for the cause of inclusion even within the context of school inspection, policy, league tables and legislation, etc. 'Effective schools manage special education needs by being clear about their priorities when allocating roles and responsibilities' (Cowne 2003: 9). But there is a caveat; and that is that in order to achieve inclusive goals, it has been suggested that schools have to exceed what are the 'normal' efforts of staff, in other words, staff have to be even more committed and work harder than their peers elsewhere. Research suggests that committed and talented heads and teachers can improve schools – even with disadvantaged pupils with SEN (Mortimore and Whitty 2000). Leadership on inclusion can be positioned within the following framework:

- vision building
- harnessing individual skills
- promoting critical thinking
- involving staff in the leadership process.

(Ainscow et al. 2000b)

However, managing change and the change process is not always easy. There can be conflict, disagreement and colleagues reluctant to embrace a culture of change. The style of leadership may directly affect the way in which

LIVERPOOL JOHN MOORES UNIVERSITY
LEARNING SERVICES

SEN and inclusion is carried forward. Increasingly there are calls for 'trans-formational' approaches that empower the school community, rather than 'transactional' styles that sustain traditional hierarchy and control (Ainscow 2002: 165). A transformational approach can lead to a position whereby the headteacher has a clear overall vision of the direction the school is taking that encourages individuality as something to be respected and celebrated. This requires 'group processes that are used to facilitate a problem-solving climate ... Leadership functions can be spread throughout the staff group' (Ainscow 2002: 127–128). However, it must be recognized that 'To do so requires leaders with sufficient confidence to expose the school's directions, functions, structures and resources, staff, student and community capacity' (Dempster 2009: 29).

In contrast to the mediated and distributed style of leadership and man-agement that would suggest potentially more 'buy-in' to the notion of the inclusive school, is the dominant, hierarchical and hands-on style implicated in some policy documents. This can result in passivity and a lack of engagement with the school's strategy. 'The elitist implication of this view is that leaders are more visionary and trustworthy than anyone else', but it does not have to be this way; examples from other countries such as Denmark suggest that beliefs and values are not disseminated from top down, rather there is a 'shared dialogue between teachers and management' (Angus 1994 quoted in Slee *et al.* 2005: 133).

With leadership clearly being a key factor in approaches to inclusion, what is required is a change of emphasis towards transformational approaches to management and leadership. This could mean a devolved form of leadership where the vision and ethos of the school are distributed, collective responsi-bility assumed and colleagues empowered. This is the antithesis of the more traditional and 'transactional' approach that operates through a bureaucratic, hierarchical and top-down system of control and surveillance. The implication here is that there may well need to be a 'concerted effort' (Ainscow 2002: 167) to deconstruct the existing organizational structures; a paradigm shift that cre-ates new roles and responsibilities. However, it has been recognized that time, resources and finance need to be in place in order to support staff development and training, thereby 'establishing a climate' for inclusion. The styles of leader-ship are encapsulated in Table 4.1.

Leadership of the school community and providing a clear steer on inclusive approaches to schooling clearly plays an important role in bringing inclusion to the fore. However, whilst this might imply a clear top-down management style, in reality it is important that this need not be the case. For measures to be effective the whole school community needs to buy in to action on inclusion and the responsibilities shared or mediated throughout the staff team. Research has suggested that it is not only the quality of leadership that is important, but the way that the majority of staff are trusted in the process of delivering on school development (Mortimore and Whitty 2000: 14).

Table 4.1 The styles of leadership

The traditional view	The emerging view
Leadership resides in individual systems	Leadership is a social property
Hierarchically based	Leadership can occur anywhere
Linked to office	
Leaders do things to followers	A complex mutual process of influence
Different from and more important than management	Leadership/management distinction unhelpful
Leaders are different	Anyone can be a leader
Leaders make a crucial difference performance	Leadership is one of many factors that influence organisational performance
Effective leadership generalisable	The context of leadership is crucial

Source: Rayner 2007: 83

Dyson *et al.*'s (2002) systematic review of school-level actions for promoting participation by all students concludes with the following themes that contribute to inclusion:

- the importance of school culture
- leadership and decision making
- structures and practices
- the policy context.

(Dyson *et al.* 2002: 45–48)

Leadership and culture remain central to school improvement, in terms of inclusion. In addition, a sense of a contributing and valued professional community is also key. Engagement with parents and the wider community outside of the school are also important (Dyson *et al.* 2002).

Other key factors (Mortimore and Whitty 2000: 14–15) in school improvement are those of the leadership stance, teamwork and the need for 'committed and talented heads and teachers'. Such an approach is an integral part of a school's response to school development planning and whole school inclusion and is reflected in the ethos of the institution. Advocates of the school improvement programme should consider 'the head teacher, staff and school governing body – having listened to the views and advice of school inspectors, consultants or researchers [and are] well placed to decide how best to improve their own institutions' (Mortimore and Whitty 2000: 12). This, of course, can be expanded to include local authority support, professionals in supporting and advisory roles, and initiatives such as *Every Child Matters*, but ultimately it requires 'distributed leadership' to influence capacity, change working conditions and increase motivation and commitment (Dempster 2009: 28–29).

However, one of the enduring problems is that 'discussions of values and the type of society to which schools articulate/adhere are ignored. Instead, effective schooling coheres with the assumed self-evidence of the discourse of the Education Reform Act and the raising standards chorus' (Slee *et al.* 2005: 111). This suggests more problematic issues than the purely pragmatic approach to inclusion of redesigning the SDP, showing leadership on inclusion and developing an ethos of diversity. Indeed, societal values represent a rather subjective construct, compared to the day-to-day decision making of how to differentiate the curriculum, or School Action programmes, or deciding on intervention strategies. Any discussion of 'values' immediately prompts the question – whose values? Society's? Parents'? Politicians'? The school senior management team's? Leading on inclusion within such a varied and unpredictable climate, which produces pressures from a wide range of interests, is demanding. Ultimately the 'assumed self-evidence' on league tables, for example, creates such an irresistible discourse, even though based on problematical methodologies, that one is straight-jacketed by the dominant ideology. Sociological perspectives tend to be critical of the ability for a school to be effective and to achieve school improvement, in the light of social, cultural, political and economic contexts (Mortimore and Whitty 2000: 18).

Conclusion

Whole school inclusion can be difficult and complex. Inclusion can be seen as an ongoing process, a journey towards an ideal, and some schools will be further along the journey than others. It may not be possible to be an inclusive school that has achieved some notional attainment for success and therefore requires no further progress; rather it is more accurate to describe schools as continually seeking to develop more inclusive practice. This process must involve the whole school community, it depends upon the understanding of and commitment to core values that then inform the development of school culture, policy and practice (Booth and Ainscow 2002). Change is therefore often small and incremental rather than wholesale. However, 'if schools do not seek actively to create an inclusive culture, then there is no point trying to develop inclusive policies' (Ekins and Grimes 2009: 133). Further, inclusive education is 'a relatively young field which inevitably lacks a well-established empirical research base' (Dyson *et al.* 2002: 59). We need to consider our role as practitioner researchers – how we develop teaching professionals and approaches that nurture and sustain evidence-based inclusion and inclusive practices that can be effective, evaluated and disseminated as good practice and supported by headteachers, governors and research bodies. As the role of the SENCO and the importance of inclusion are increasingly recognized, the onus will be on all who actively practice inclusion to demonstrate effective strategies to their communities of practice. Dyson *et al.*'s report (2002: 60) calls for 'a greater willingness to test claims of inclusivity' and suggests:

> The literature is filled with empirical claims that 'inclusive' schools, for instance, have particular characteristics or that particular classroom practices lead to greater student participation, or that particular change processes lead schools to greater inclusivity. Where such empirical claims are made, they need to be tested empirically.
>
> (Dyson *et al.* 2002: 59)

Evidence suggests that progress is possible in the light of other pressures. The

> possibilities for inclusive development are inherent in all schools and are realised in often quite unexceptional and unpromising circumstances ... some more widespread move in an inclusive direction is possible ... such a move might result from supporting the incremental development of schools rather than from a radical transformation of understandings and practices.
>
> (Ainscow *et al.* 2006b: 305)

It is reasonable to conclude, even acknowledging competing tensions and values, that progress can be made through effective leadership and a clear, practical vision mediated through the SDP. 'Tensions' are clearly evident and 'dissonance' occurs when standards and inclusion run parallel (Dyson *et al.* 2002, drawing on Thomas and Loxely) and as a result a paradox presents itself. However, there are calls for pragmatism, suggesting that progress towards inclusion can be made at local and school level. Policy directives suggest interpretation and compromise, from everyone including 'civil servants to local administrators to teachers' (Thomas and Loxley 2007: 107 and Chapter 6). This 'pragmatism' must also be mediated through the SDP in ways that are easily understood and colleagues will buy in to.

The metaphor of the 'journey' for school improvement is a useful one. It reminds us that we are all at different junctures on a route and may never reach the destination, as schools and society adapt and change to the will and demands of each new generation. Leading on inclusion requires vision, but also a pragmatic and utilitarian need to consider the following phases on the 'school improvement journey':

- Where are we now?
- Where do we want to be?
- How will we get there?
- What do we need to do?
- Where will we go next?

(Ainscow 1994)

The question one then seems condemned to repeatedly ask is how much inclusion can one achieve within the standards agenda, which is often presented as a fait accompli? The culture of exam performance, league tables and teaching to the test means that the inclusion agenda is too often eclipsed by competing pressures, with little room for manoeuvre. Practitioners need to make space for inclusion but the danger is always that it is 'a bit of an add on' or that it is 'slipping off' people's agendas (Ainscow 2002: 209). With the new UK Coalition Government elected in 2010, this approach will probably remain.

All of this paints a rather depressing picture. However, research has suggested that a positive and real difference can be made in terms of school improvement *and* attainment for all. That there are reasons to believe that, through raising standards *and* improving performance, the quality of education for all create benefits not just for the mainstream, but for those who are marginalized and disadvantaged.

In practical terms, there are actions that enable the inclusive approach to take shape and which can be prompted by the SDP, for example a thorough audit of the school's capacity to lead on inclusion, a review of pedagogy and the curriculum, pupils' achievements, resources and real estate, to name but a few. However, no one should be under an illusion: there exists a 'complex web of influences' (Mortimore and Whitty 2000: 13) at play in this process. While the school can do many things within its power to present an inclusive ethos, the standards agenda will impose itself to such an extent that it may offset the school's efforts on inclusive practice. Within the context of a neoliberal agenda in terms of the marketization of education, combined with resolute structural barriers such as class and the 'othering' of race and disability, to what extent can leading on inclusion bring about change in a school's outlook? Such a daunting question might seem overwhelming, but maybe through a clear ethos, leadership that is inspiring, devolved responsibilities through communities of practice and a focused SDP with inclusion as a core value, then it is possible that, incrementally at least, progress can be made.

If you are based in a school setting, you might like to consider the following:

Reflective Activity

- Is the management process of your school top down?
- Or is it a more democratic style where responsibilities are shared across the school's communities of practice?
- How might developing new styles of leadership and management facilitate or act as a barrier to inclusion in the context of your own institution?

Or

Critically examine your school's SDP. Ask yourself:

- To what extent is inclusion strategy incorporated, compared to other demands?
- To what extent is inclusion prioritised within the SDP?
- How does the SDP facilitate inclusionary practice?
- What measures are in place to record improvement?

(Ainscow *et al.* 2006b: 296)

Chapter 5

The importance of a whole school culture of inclusion

Alison Ekins

Introduction

The effective co-ordination of provision is a central process within all schools, and one which can often be segmented and marginalised, leading to inefficient or ineffective planning and provision. This chapter takes an approach to co-ordinating provision and meeting the needs of pupils with special educational needs (SEN) which is centrally based upon inclusive principles. The key message is that for systems and processes to be effective for meeting the needs of pupils with SEN, they should be seen as whole school systems: systems to meet the needs of all pupils, rather than just those which we 'do for pupils with SEN'.

This is a key shift in thinking, and involves a deeper consideration of the importance and impact of shared inclusive values and cultures within our schools. This chapter draws on recent research (Ekins 2010) which emphasises the centrality of these processes and demonstrates how this will impact positively upon an approach to co-ordinating provision which will lead to improved outcomes for all pupils.

The final part of this chapter will then provide and describe a model to illustrate how an effective whole school approach can be developed which will enable whole staff responsibility and commitment to the processes, ensuring that the needs of all pupils are meet.

Co-ordinating provision effectively: what does this mean?

For many years, schools have been required and expected to carefully monitor pupil progress and plan provision to ensure that the needs of all pupils are being monitored and met (Ofsted 2004, 2006, 2011; DCSF 2007c, 2008a). Over recent years, therefore, schools have become familiar with a range of systems linked to this system. These include:

- pupil tracking data
- data analysis

- identification of need
- intervention planning
- provision mapping
- pupil progress review meetings
- target setting
- self-evaluation.

In recent years, with the Labour Government education policy and the National Strategies, there has been an increasing focus on prescribed intervention programmes and materials, with the expectation that where underachievement is identified, pupils would be able to access booster, catch-up or intensive intervention support to meet their needs.

This has helped to emphasise the issue of needing to provide 'additional to and different from' provision for pupils, and has helped to embed a notion that this provision is not just for pupils with identified special educational needs, but also for those pupils who are underachieving, or have fallen behind and are simply in need of some short-term support. However, as the following section will unpick further, to be able to really meet the needs of pupils and co-ordinate provision effectively, it is not just about the implementation of a particular intervention programme or strategy. Rather, the implementation of interventions needs to be underpinned by whole school commitment to and understanding of inclusive values and principles, and practice needs to be embedded within a whole school approach to co-ordinating provision. Where the needs of pupils are not effectively being met, there is often a disjointed approach to these processes or a haphazard approach to deciding upon what type of support or provision is required.

If you are based in a school setting, you might like to take some time to complete the following reflective activity, before reading on. This will help you to capture and review existing practice in your own setting, and will help you to engage in a more informed review and reconsideration of practice at the end of the chapter.

Reflective Activity

Which of the following processes do you currently use in your school context?

- pupil tracking data
- data analysis
- identification of need
- intervention planning
- provision mapping

- pupil progress review meetings
- target setting
- self-evaluation.

How are they used?

Who takes responsibility for the different processes?

How do they directly impact upon the educational experience of the pupil?

How effective is this?

In the final section of the chapter, the discussions about the *Inclusion in Action* model (Ekins and Grimes 2009) will present case studies about different schools at different stages of development, and the benefits and limitations of each of those stages for the effective meeting of pupil needs. You will be able to compare your initial review with features identified through the case studies, to help you in planning future development work in your school setting.

What is inclusion? The importance of inclusive cultures and values

Developing inclusive practices within schools is a complicated process: it is not simply about the introduction of a new system or piece of paper. Instead, building teaching practices to respond to the needs of all pupils, including those with complex or challenging SEN, is a highly emotive business. This is something that is often overlooked by government policy and local authority or school practice.

In recent years, the education system has become overrun with new initiatives. Schools and teachers have been overloaded trying to respond to the latest initiative or strategy to emerge from the National Strategies, or the latest educational trend, such as the emergence of synthetic phonics as the dominant way to teach reading and phonics in schools. So much time has been devoted to slavishly following the latest piece of guidance from the government that time has been lost or taken away from the fundamental business of reflection within schools. In this respect, the professional identity of teachers and senior leaders working hard in schools has been undermined. A system has emerged where teachers have become accustomed (or perhaps trained) not to think and reflect themselves but instead to follow an overprescriptive curriculum, which includes scripted intervention programmes. Perhaps this is too harsh: an overstatement of the reality perhaps. Of course, there have always been highly committed and motivated teachers who will question and reflect rather than just following prescribed programmes, however, we do need to consider carefully the implications and impact of recent policy directives upon the direction of practice within our schools.

At this time of change it is important to acknowledge the recent history of teaching practices in our schools: to consider the impact that this de-professionalisation of teachers has had upon the potential development of inclusive practices in schools, and to consider new ways forward for the future.

The Coalition Government seems to recognise this. The White Paper *The Importance of Teaching* (DfE 2010) emphasises the need to move away from government diktat for the sake of it, instead proposing a model which places trust in the professional and moral responsibility of teachers. Schools are therefore promised 'decisive action to free our teachers from constraint and improve their professional status and authority' (DfE 2010: 8). This new model specifically recognises the 'moral purpose and desire to help children and young people succeed' which is embedded within teachers and headteachers, and promises to place greater trust and respect in that rather than continuing 'unnecessary prescription and bureaucracy' (DfE 2010: 28).

While these are heartening words, we wait to see how this will be achieved in reality as the Coalition Government's policies take effect in schools. However, what we can see is growing evidence and understanding that an effective whole school approach to co-ordinating provision is centred upon a whole staff understanding of inclusive principles, rather than the simple implementation of a particular approach or intervention.

Central to this new, more effective approach are some key underpinning principles:

- understanding inclusion as an emotive subject and the impact of inclusion upon teacher self-identity
- developing a collaborative whole staff approach built upon inclusive staff relationships
- understanding and defining shared inclusive principles.

Understanding inclusion as an emotive subject

Teaching is a deeply personal and moral endeavour, highly charged with emotional attachment and engagement (Nias *et al.* 1989; Woods *et al.* 1997; Day 2004), with a 'significant and ongoing part of being a teacher [being] the experiencing and management of strong emotions' (Day *et al.* 2006: 612). On top of this, inclusion is a very complex concept, which can be an emotionally charged issue for different staff within the school setting. As the emotively entitled *Cost of Inclusion* study (MacBeath *et al.* 2006) concluded, while many teachers do view inclusion in a positive way, there is an underlying sense that inclusion as a principle has made the task of teaching more difficult:

> Increasing the range of needs and abilities within the 'mainstream' classroom has had a major impact on the nature and balance of teachers' work. The presence of even one child with complex needs without relevant support and resourcing could be enough to upset the balance and flow of teaching and learning for all.
>
> (MacBeath *et al.* 2006: 62)

Responding to the daily challenges of meeting the needs of pupils with high levels of complex or challenging needs can be very undermining to the teacher's professional identity:

> Inability to meet the range of need leaves many teachers with a sense of guilt, worrying that they are letting down both the children with special needs, who they feel inadequately skilled to deal with as well as the rest of the class whom they are denying attention.
>
> (ibid.)

It can then become easy for the teacher to blame the pupil for the challenges they present, rather than examining and removing the wider barriers impacting upon the pupil. This may include needing to recognise that existing teaching approaches are not fully appropriate to meet the needs of pupils within the particular class group, and requiring a review and development of new teaching approaches to meet needs. The intense impact of emotion upon staff groups striving to develop inclusive practice therefore needs to be explicitly recognised and acknowledged by senior leaders. Indeed, the terminology within this study – 'strain', 'pressure', 'disruption', 'marginalisation', 'concerns', 'guilt', 'litigation', 'lack of resources' and 'insufficient expertise' highlights the complex and highly emotive nature of developing inclusive practices in schools (MacBeath *et al.* 2006).

Recent research within two case study schools (Ekins 2010) also highlights the impact of emotional responses upon the overall experience of developing inclusive practices in schools. While it had been expected that the research would show that schools develop inclusive practices in different ways, related to the different approaches and practices that they put in place, what emerged as the significant finding was the centrality of emotion, and linked to that the development of a culture of shared understanding and close staff relationships in developing inclusive practices.

The quotations below, from teachers working in two schools with high numbers of pupils with complex needs, highlight the intensely emotional experience of developing inclusive practices:

At first I dreaded coming into school.

I came here and hated it with a passion.

It got to the point where I was really unable to cope.

I lost the will to live.

Like a living nightmare.

Soul destroying.

Emotional responses were not used as an excuse to perpetuate exclusionary practices. Instead, within both schools, they were explicitly acknowledged and used as a resource to support the development of shared inclusive values and close working relationships within an inclusive culture of collaborative problem-sharing rather than individual responsibility. Indeed, even when the teachers were stretched to their limits and were starting to question their professional identity, they were still able to see the underpinning inclusive values and reasons for the work that they were doing with the pupils. The quotations that emerged from the research data highlighted the complex nature of developing inclusive practices in terms of the mixed emotional responses that this provokes:

Actually it's very extreme, there's probably no middle ground, we cope really well, or we think that was a complete disaster.

It certainly has been a challenge ... but very rewarding as well – I look forward to coming to school.

Working in the school has been horrendous ... but it's been a huge huge learning curve, I wouldn't change it for the world.

Whilst initially I dreaded coming into school ... I've found it immensely satisfying.

Developing inclusive practices within these schools was therefore considered in terms of their moral responsibility to 'make a difference' to their pupils. This was the driving force shared by all staff working within the school and it was noticeable during the research period that if there were staff who were not fully committed to those shared principles, then they left the school and new staff replaced them.

Developing a collaborative whole staff approach built upon inclusive staff relationships

The inclusive cultures in these two schools were deeply embedded and supported the teachers in responding to challenging needs. This was evidenced in the way that the teachers worked with each other, which was considered to be 'special' and 'different' to the ways of working that teachers had experienced in other school settings. There was an embedded ethos of supporting each other, of valuing each other's expertise, acknowledging that no one had all of the answers and solutions and that it was not a problem to need to ask for help. Staff in the two schools highlighted the 'professional dialogue and support between the adults in the school' and the opportunity to 'talk through the challenges and come up with a new idea'.

The staff relationships in the schools were relaxed, informal and collegial. Across the whole school environment, from the staff room to the classroom, there was informal respect for each other and an open collaborative approach to supporting each other. This included professional discussions about how to meet the needs of pupils, as well as informal social arrangements.

Understanding and defining shared inclusive principles

Key to developing a shared approach to meeting needs is therefore an embedded inclusive culture: one built upon shared inclusive values. Thus, 'Inclusion can only work in a culture of collaboration in which there is sharing of resource and expertise' (MacBeath *et al.* 2006: 67).

Reflective Activity

What are the inclusive values embedded within your school setting?

How and when are they explicitly discussed and reviewed?

Do you think that everyone (staff, pupils, parents, the wider community) are aware of them?

How important do you think that inclusive values may be for the development of your school?

Are there any tensions or competing priorities impacting upon shared values within the school setting?

How could these be resolved?

How do the inclusive values impact directly upon practice and the educational experiences of pupils?

How do the inclusive values impact upon the image of the school experienced by staff members, pupils, parents, the wider community?

How important do you think this is?

Inclusive values and principles can be difficult to define, and there can be tensions between values or priorities held by different staff members within the same school. The seeming tension between the recent Labour Government priorities of standards and inclusion is an obvious one to highlight. The focus on raising standards may have impacted upon the desire and motivation of some schools to include those pupils with SEN who may impact upon whole school standards but this is a simplistic reading of the situation. Research by Black-Hawkins *et al.* (2007) has identified that developing inclusive practices for all can positively support the raising of standards, and a focus on raising standards can also impact upon the ability for schools to positively include pupils with more diverse needs, through their person-centred approach to meeting individual needs.

Within this chapter, the term 'developing inclusive practices' is used as this reflects the belief that inclusion is not a pre-determined destination (Mittler 2000): rather, it is a never-ending journey or process of whole school development. Here, 'inclusive practices' refers to the removal of barriers to learning and participation for ALL pupils: it is not just about pupils with SEN. However, where the particular needs of each individual are identified, valued and addressed, the needs of pupils with SEN can be more effectively met. Such an approach helps to take processes and practices to support the needs of pupils with SEN away from the sidelines: from something that an identified individual – the Special Educational Needs Co-ordinator (SENCO) has to address – to something that is part of a whole school inclusive approach to meeting the needs of all pupils. This is the most effective way to improve outcomes and participation for all pupils, including those with SEN.

A very broad way to define inclusion, taken from the *Index for Inclusion* (Booth and Ainscow 2002), may therefore be helpful in supporting schools to reconsider the inclusive values underpinning their own school context, to:

- reduce barriers to learning
- increase participation and access to learning
- support diversity.

Reflective Activity

Take each of the inclusive principles in turn and think about the questions on the next page:

- reduce barriers to learning
- increase participation and access to learning
- support diversity.

What do you already do in your own practice to address each of those principles?

What impact does this have upon your pupils, and particularly upon pupils with SEN?

What whole school systems or approaches are in place to meet each of those principles?

How have they been agreed?

How effective are they?

Are there any other inclusive principles that you think would be fundamental for the effective development of practice in your school?

A whole school approach to co-ordinating provision within an inclusive approach to meeting needs

The effective co-ordination of provision to meet the needs of pupils with SEN is not simply about knowledge and implementation of a particular strategy: it must be embedded within consistent and agreed whole school inclusive values, principles and practices. Building upon this foundation, the co-ordination of provision utilising a whole school approach based upon inclusive principles can be achieved and can have significant impact upon the participation, progress and outcomes for not only pupils with SEN, but ALL pupils.

The *Inclusion in Action* model (Ekins and Grimes 2009) provides a framework for reconsidering practice and helps practitioners to understand how the co-ordination of provision moves away from the simple setting up of separate systems, into becoming a dynamic integrated model of whole school development. The *Inclusion in Action* model is centrally positioned upon three underpinning principles:

1   inclusion
2   school development
3   self evaluation.

These principles link in dynamic ways to enable significant school change which is focused upon ensuring that all pupils are provided with a learning environment within which they can participate and progress. The *Inclusion in Action* model is directly concerned with the understanding and acknowledgement of the complex emotive nature of inclusive school development, the development of collaborative staff practices and the sharing of inclusive values, as outlined earlier in the chapter. Upon this foundation of key principles, the following individual processes involved in co-ordinating provision are seen not as separate systems, but as part of a dynamic model, where each part of the process directly impacts upon the effectiveness of another:

- pupil tracking data
- data analysis
- identification of need
- intervention planning
- provision mapping
- pupil progress review meetings
- target setting
- self-evaluation.

As the model in Figure 5.1 represents, all aspects of co-ordinating provision are dynamically linked to each other, showing the impact that they have upon the development of an effective and meaningful system. Data tracking and analysis, for example, is not seen as a separate process. Instead, it is dynamically linked to the setting of targets and the co-ordination and implementation of provision and interventions, underpinned by all staff self-evaluation, shared inclusive values and a strategic approach to whole school development. This model of practice explicitly emphasises the importance of whole staff ownership. It is

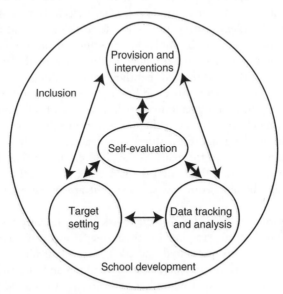

Figure 5.1 Identifying and removing barriers to learning

Source: Ekins and Grimes (2009)

not about one person (traditionally the SENCO) completing all the tasks her/himself. Instead, it is about providing a framework within which all staff in the school setting can develop professional dialogue about effective ways to meet the needs of all pupils, and develop meaningful and effective ways to record this to support the ongoing monitoring, review and evaluation of pupil progress.

The case studies below provide information about schools at the different stages of development leading to the *Inclusion in Action* model. These case studies are based upon our research working in and with schools over the past six years (Ekins and Grimes 2009). The case studies provide a powerful tool for supporting the review and development of school practice, helping practitioners to identify elements of their own practice and relate it to a developmental model of whole school practice.

Case Study 1

In this school (School 1) most of the processes are used, although they do not happen in any formalised way. Staff do not use pupil progress review meetings. Most of the processes are completed by members of staff in leadership positions, and there is very little, if any, connection between the work and analysis that they do of the processes and development of day-to-day teaching practice. Generally, teaching staff are asked to provide information, for example assessment week data, or information relating to the identification of needs within the class, and then this is separately processed by the individual member of the leadership team. Feedback is not given, and teachers are unaware of the purpose and implications of the information that they are providing.

Interventions are set up in an ad hoc way to respond to the individual class teacher, and their preferences or knowledge of different interventions. In one class/department there is a teacher who is very interested in speech and language difficulties, and detailed speech and language programmes are set up for many of the children in her class. It is unfortunate, however, that there are pupils in other areas of the school who would really benefit from this support, but are not supported by this teacher.

Members of the leadership team work independently to gather the information that they require for their roles. Once the information is gathered it is neatly presented and filed in separate files. Time is not allocated for discussion and feedback of the trends and information being gathered. This means that whole school patterns of need are not identified and co-ordinated effectively.

Case Study 2

In this school (School 2), the systems are all used. There is a senior leadership team with clearly defined roles and responsibilities and together these members of staff co-ordinate approaches to provision and meeting need across the school. Data and information is gathered from the range of teaching staff at regular periods through the school year, and the senior leadership team has developed a good approach to scrutinising the information to enable identification of whole school trends and patterns of need. They are able to use this information to collectively plan approaches to whole school development.

This information and analysis is however not shared with the other teaching staff, who are therefore unaware of the rationale for resource deployment, including the allocation of support staff through the school. Class and subject teachers also have no process for requesting or setting up more individualised intervention programmes to meet the needs of pupils within their classes. Instead, a full timetable of interventions has been designed by the senior leadership team to incorporate all of the key literacy and numeracy interventions.

Pupil progress review meetings have just started to be used and are attended by all of the members of the senior leadership team as well as the class or subject teacher. The meeting is led by the senior leadership team, who focus the discussions on analysing underachievement within the class group. No time in the meeting is spent upon collaborative problem solving and planning for appropriate and meaningful interventions and support to respond to those needs in innovative and creative ways.

There is some impact of these systems upon the day-to-day educational experience of pupils, although too many pupils' individual needs are being missed as there is not enough collaborative discussion of needs involving the class or subject teachers who know the pupils best.

Case Study 3

This school (School 3) has developed a whole school approach to co-ordinating provision, where all the processes are fully owned and used by all teachers. Each year, time is prioritised on the school development plan to enable the whole staff to review the effectiveness of the systems: including how useful they are, whether the formats are still being used, whether additional information needs to be added to any of the formats. In this school, the senior leadership team ensure that the processes that have been set up are used and applied to meet the needs of all pupils. Therefore, provision mapping, intervention planning and target setting are processes used to support all pupils. This has meant that the processes have not become marginalised. They are not just something that has to be done for a few pupils with SEN in the class group. Instead, the processes form a central part of the role of the teacher in planning day-to-day educational experiences that are relevant and meaningful and directly relate to the pupil's individual learning needs.

In this school, the processes are seen as linked. Rather than a number of separate processes, the school has set up a central process for co-ordinating provision, which involves all the separate elements. This has helped all staff to understand the connections between, and relevance of, each piece of information or process for impacting upon the effective overall co-ordination of provision. Teachers and pupils are the central owners and users of the process, and are therefore fundamental in the use and development of all the system. This ensures the relevance of the system as a whole, and the direct impact upon all day-to-day educational experiences.

Reflective Activity

Having read the case studies above, where would you position your own school practice?

What works well in your own school currently?

What needs to be further developed in order to reach a system which is similar to that described under School 3?

How can you achieve this?

Are there any barriers to be overcome?

What are these, and how could these be overcome, taking into consideration the earlier discussions about the importance of an embedded inclusive culture and values?

The case studies are presented here to mirror the information that you identified about your own school practice (if appropriate) in the reflective activity at the beginning of the chapter. It will be useful for you to directly compare your reflections with the information presented below to help you to explore ways to further develop whole school practice within your own school setting. These case studies can also be used as a whole staff development tool, to stimulate group discussion about elements of school practice.

Where do we go from here?

For the twenty-first century we need to continue to strive for the development of school systems and understandings of meeting the needs of all pupils which are founded upon inclusive principles. Inclusion does not just relate to pupils with SEN or to provision and practice. Rather, it should entail a principled approach to meeting the needs of all pupils, based upon the central principle of 'removing barriers to learning and participation' (Booth and Ainscow 2002).

For practices and systems to more effectively meet the needs of pupils with SEN, we need to foster and embed whole school approaches, taking SEN systems away from the sidelines and into the mainstream. It is in this way that we will be able to provide a more responsive approach to meeting the needs of all pupils, one where the whole school takes responsibility for meeting those needs. The *Inclusion in Action* model (Ekins and Grimes 2009) discussed and presented above, provides a framework for embedding the essential consideration of inclusive values, principles and practices within traditionally taken-for-granted paper-based systems. This effectively transforms thinking and practice in the school, moving the co-ordination of provision away from being a separated and segregated task, into becoming a meaningful whole school process embedded upon strong shared inclusive values and practices. Such an approach to co-ordinating provision does much to acknowledge and support the individual teacher in responding to what can at times be the emotive and challenging task of providing inclusive practices to meet the needs of all pupils. The *Inclusion in Action* model emphasises a collaborative approach to meeting needs, shifting the focus away from individual class teacher responsibility into an approach where the whole school works together to follow systems and processes which are genuinely shared and collectively owned.

Conclusion

This chapter has considered the issue of co-ordinating provision effectively, an issue which is of key significance to the effective education of pupils with SEN. However, it has considered this issue not just in terms of the application of a particular approach and not just in terms of pupils with SEN. Instead, this chapter has positioned the co-ordination of provision within an approach to whole school inclusive development. It has therefore emphasised key issues impacting upon practitioner understanding of developing inclusive practices, including the emotional impact upon teacher self-identity, the importance of collaborative staff practices and the development and articulation of shared inclusive values. The *Inclusion in Action* model (Ekins and Grimes 2009) has been used as a framework to support the reconsideration of understanding about how to co-ordinate provision effectively, while the accompanying case studies have provided a tool through which practitioners can re-examine and develop existing practices.

Chapter 6

Learning and teaching in inclusive classrooms

Bridget Middlemas

Introduction

This chapter will discuss the possibilities and challenges posed for teaching and support staff who are responsible for learning and teaching in inclusive classrooms, and considers the potential benefits that may follow for all students with special educational needs (SEN) or disabilities who are educated in such a setting. Some key points from the inclusion/exclusion and mainstream/segregation debates will be discussed.

A well-planned, truly inclusive classroom will be able to welcome all students, including those who do not have English (in English schools) as their first language, children from socially deprived backgrounds or those who are returning to school after time spent in hospital. Yet, agreeing what 'educational inclusion' looks like in the classroom is not a straightforward process and many of our current definitions and understandings of educational inclusion are contested.

Various aspects of educational inclusion from a classroom design perspective will also be highlighted, in terms of the learners as well as those who support learning. Sections include designing for inclusion; listening to the student voice; staffing and teamwork issues; organising groups and classes; and the necessity of providing other spaces in the school to support inclusive learning and teaching.

Issues affecting learning and teaching in inclusive classrooms

Mainstream school staff and those in segregated settings are required to have a working knowledge of a sometimes bewildering range of recommendations, statutory guidance documents, good practice guidelines and educational legislation, coming from a diverse range of government departments (such as the Department for Education, the Department of Health, Ofsted and the Audit Commission). Additionally they may find themselves considering learning and teaching recommendations from a variety of non-governmental organisations such as the British Dyslexia Association (for example, *Dyslexia Friendly Schools* 2010) or the Foundation for People with Learning Disabilities (*What about us?* 2008). Mainstream inclusion for learners with SEN and disabilities has gradually become more commonplace over the past twenty years or so. The Special Educational Needs and Disability Act (2001) (SENDA) extended the right of pupils with learning difficulties or disabilities to be educated in mainstream schools or units, unless this would prove to be incompatible with the efficient education of other children, or the parents specifically wished their child to attend a special school. The statutory guidance *Inclusive Schooling* recommended that nearly all children with SEN should be successfully taught in a mainstream setting (DfES 2001b). Three years later, the government's strategy for SEN, *Removing Barriers to Achievement*, also supported the move towards greater inclusion, at the same time acknowledging the challenges involved in such a systemic move (DfES 2004a).

As a result of the universal changes that have taken place in the education system over the past few years, many working definitions of educational inclusion have emerged – each one with its own nuances according to which political, philosophical, moral or educational source it has been derived from. Some definitions appear to originate from the deficit or medical model of SEN, attempting to measure 'difference' in relation to a perceived normality or status quo, such as the *Code of Practice* (DfES 2001a). Other definitions (such as the Special Educational Needs and Disability Act 2001 or the Council for Disabled Children's *Inclusion Policy* 2008) arise from a more politically oriented *human rights perspective*, and are fundamentally rights-based approaches focusing on the rights of the individual learner. Armstrong *et al.* (2000) note that, at the heart of the inclusive education debate, serious issues such as human rights, equal opportunities and social justice are commonly at the forefront of discussions. Tilstone *et al.* (2002: 2) observe that support for inclusive schooling is an increasingly important component of UK government education policies, with an emphasis on 'strong educational, social and moral grounds' for children with SEN and disabilities to be educated in mainstream schools. In the UK the range of legislation and statutory guidance affecting students with SEN or disabilities who are being 'included' or 'excluded' is often problematic for classroom-based staff, as different sets of legislation and guidelines affect different groups of learners. The sometimes confusing overlaps between disability legislation, SEN statutory guidance and SEN/disability good practice guidelines can be seen in Figure 6.1.

Some initiatives have attempted to address the critical issue of overlap in some detail, such as the practical 2006 publication, *Implementing the Disability Discrimination Act in Schools and Early Years Settings*, published jointly by the Department for Education and Skills and the Disability Rights Commission (2006). This publication acknowledges that many mainstream schools are now rising to the challenge of developing inclusive classrooms, where the majority of learners with SEN and disabled learners will be encouraged to attend. They recommend that the following points are addressed in order to cater for a wide range of abilities and needs:

- a welcoming and supportive ethos in all areas of the school
- a positive, 'can do' attitude from staff and management
- good working relationships with outside agencies and multi-disciplinary teams
- forward planning and strong leadership
- the use of expertise from outside the school
- ongoing and regular consultations with pupils and parents
- effective staff training opportunities for all staff
- regular review and evaluation of reasonable adjustments.

(DfES and DRC 2006)

Yet, are any of these recommendations really feasible? Armstrong argues that some of the UK's current SEN legislation goes little further than redressing 'the traditional deficit-driven discourse of special educational needs in the fashionable but illusionary language of inclusion' and that recent 'inclusive educational policy (in the UK) has been to forward a process of assimilation based upon an uncritical view of "normality", itself structured by the values of performativity that legitimate state regulation and control' (Armstrong 2005: 149).

In the midst of this discourse, it is worth noting that mainstream placements for learners with SEN and disabilities have been increasing on an annual basis in the UK since 2003. For example, in 2007, there were only around 11,000 students with SEN in England who were *not* being educated in mainstream settings (Audit Commission 2007) and that the financial benefits

Figure 6.1 Issues affecting learning and teaching in inclusive classrooms

of inclusion versus segregation often cause confusion among budget holders. In the Audit Commission's 2007 report *Out of authority placements for special educational needs*, it emerged that many local authorities were unaware of the exact costs per student of either local or out-of-authority packages of support, and often had little understanding of the out-of-authority providers' costs. They also concluded that:

> while strategic planning for the educational needs of children with complex needs has improved, opportunities to provide more integrated and cost-effective services through joint working between education, social care and health services are not being maximised.
>
> (Audit Commission 2007: 2)

To some, the notion of 'integrated and cost-effective services' might simply be seen as an excuse for local authorities to save substantial amounts of money by providing local education on one campus, and under the care of one Special Educational Needs Co-ordinator (SENCO), rather than providing the specialist support needed for some groups of children (for example those with chronic medical conditions, or those with challenging behaviour). Others argue that, in spite of these concerns, there is still a strong argument for designing all our school buildings and the learning spaces within them in the most accessible and inclusive way, in order that an increasing number of children can be successfully educated alongside their neighbours and relatives, rather than having to make a journey to another part of town, or to spend weekdays in a residential setting many miles from home.

However, the growing awareness that more children are now attending mainstream placements has led to an understandable apprehension from some teaching and support staff, who often complain that they feel unqualified to teach groups of children that they might never have previously encountered, nor received any specific training to teach (Brackenreed 2008; Moran and Abbott 2002). A recent survey of 25 SENCOs attending the MA programme at Roehampton University identified the following concerns in terms of their own strategic roles in promoting and supporting inclusive learning and teaching environments:

- there is not always a sufficient budget to make more than the minimum changes necessary
- many staff continue to have low expectations of some learners with SEN and disabled learners, and stereotypes are often hard to dispel
- it is essential that the head and senior management team are fully supportive of the SENCO's efforts to improve inclusive practice
- there are frequently severe time constraints on SENCOs, many of whom have a heavy teaching timetable as well as being expected to manage the administration related to their roles

- pressure from the parents of children who do not have SEN or are not disabled may cause tensions, especially when discussing examination subjects (e.g. GCSE teaching) and league tables
- some of the existing accommodation is completely unsuitable for certain groups of learners.

(Middlemas 2010)

These are not minor concerns, and the current pace of educational change does little to allay anxieties expressed by some teaching staff (see also Brackenreed 2008; Kozik *et al.* 2009; Richards and Armstrong 2010; Wedell 2009). Indeed, the very definition of the word 'inclusive' may prove daunting, for example as outlined in UNESCO's *Inclusion Toolkit*:

> 'Inclusive' does include children with disabilities, such as children who have difficulties in seeing or hearing, who cannot walk, or who are slower to learn. However, inclusive also means including ALL children who are left out of or excluded from school and from learning. These children may not speak the language of the classroom; are at risk of dropping out because they are sick, hungry, or not achieving well; or belong to a different religion or caste. They also may be girls who are pregnant ... and (those) who should be in school but are not, especially those who work ... Inclusive means that as teachers, we have the responsibility to seek out all available support (from school authorities, the community, families, children, educational institutions, health services, community leaders, and so on) for ... teaching ALL children.
>
> (UNESCO 2005: 2)

The second part of this chapter will address how we might approach some of the professional challenges highlighted in the UNESCO definition, and at the same time reflect on some examples of good practice where teaching teams have worked together to enhance learning and teaching in inclusive classrooms. In this discussion, 'classroom' will mean any part of the school where teaching takes place – including the ICT suite, a nurture group room, the science laboratories or the school library.

What do we mean by inclusive classrooms?

The importance of meeting not only the academic but also the social, emotional and sometimes medical needs of learners is now being discussed more openly in many schools, with an increased emphasis on a learner-centred rather than a teacher-centred approach. The discussion is finally moving away from 'No way, I'm not having him/her in my classroom' to 'How can I best meet his/her educational needs in our inclusive school?' For example, Kumar emphasises the importance of 'putting the needs of my students at the forefront of my classroom rather than letting the course content be the dominant presence in my class' (Kumar 2010: 5). This is a simple point, but sometimes overlooked in the busy school setting.

An increasing number of disabled students are now attending mainstream schools, often encouraged by disability organisations such as the Council for Disabled Children (CDC), who are fully supportive of any policies and practices that promote educational inclusion for disabled children. The CDC argues that:

> with the right ethos, attitude and support, many more disabled children could be included into mainstream settings. This would be to their benefit and to the benefit of their non-disabled peers … the qualities that make settings high quality inclusive settings also make them high quality settings for all children. There are excellent examples of mainstream settings including disabled children with a wide range of impairments. CDC supports policies and practices that increase the capacity of all mainstream settings to become as inclusive as the best. The best is always evolving.
>
> (Morgan and Byers 2008: 2)

The CDC's pertinent use of the word 'evolving' is a reminder of how many diverse organisations are working together for change, and at the same time acknowledging that educational inclusion is a complex process of sustained development rather than a sudden sea change. An effective inclusive classroom may be in a mainstream or a segregated setting, and some children may have a dual registration at two schools in order to provide the most appropriate placement.

Designing for inclusion

The importance of providing and funding physically accessible school buildings has always been a major part of the inclusion/exclusion and mainstream/segregation debates, with schools proudly evidencing their accessibility by the provision of ramps at the main entrance, so-called 'disabled toilets', or lifts to upstairs teaching areas. Yet many schools still fail to consider how classroom and school design can transform inclusive learning and teaching provision, especially for children with 'hidden' disabilities such as specific learning difficulties or autism. The DCSF publication *Designing for Disabled Children and Children with Special Educational Needs* (2009) was one of the first major UK publications to acknowledge the importance of classroom as well as whole school design issues relating to inclusive learning and teaching. It was compiled with assistance and advice from mainstream as well as segregated settings, and provides an excellent starting point for schools wishing to design their learning and teaching spaces in a more inclusive and fully accessible way. It brings together good practice ideas from a refreshing range of professional standpoints, including educationalists, architects, ICT and technology specialists, as well as acknowledging the views of a range of teachers and students. The guidance highlights the importance of:

- good access to buildings and facilities
- making effective use of available space/designing for flexibility and adaptability
- considering the accommodation needs of support staff and visiting professionals
- enhancing learning through effective classroom design
- good use of ICT and assistive technologies
- sensory awareness/acoustics/lighting
- health and well-being for staff and students
- safety and security issues
- sustainability/cost effectiveness
- effective staff training
- working closely with all stakeholders, and listening to the 'student voice'.

(DCSF 2009: 5)

By paying attention to the principles of inclusive design, the authors argue that those with SEN and disabilities can be enabled to participate much more fully in life at school as well as in their local community. The Foundation for People with Learning Disabilities has also been addressing a number of issues relating to inclusive design, and in 2008 carried out a major action research project involving SEN and disabled students in the UK. They found that the students often had:

strong and original views on a range of issues relating to their education. These include their environment, their own safety, having a say in school councils, accessibility, their own learning … they have the potential to generate real improvements in their schools and colleges.

(Morgan and Byers 2008: 4)

Morgan and Byers also highlight the fact that, although the student voice approach has become increasingly popular in the past ten to 15 years or so, many learners still complain that their views are not being listened to by those in authority, in spite of the recommendations made under Article 12 of the *Convention on the Rights of the Child* (UN 1989), which maintains that the state should 'assure to the child who is capable of forming his or her own views the right to express those views freely in all matters affecting the child, the views of the child being given due weight in accordance with the age and maturity of the child' (Morgan and Byers 2008: 2). The student voice approach can be used very successfully when considering inclusion, as discussed in the next section.

Listening to the student voice

The *SEN Code of Practice* (DfES 2001a) stresses the importance of actively seeking the 'voice' of learners, and using data from interviews or questionnaires to enhance and improve professional practice. This is of fundamental importance in an inclusive learning and teaching environment, and research in this field indicates that learners of all ages can make a valuable contribution to inclusive practice (Jones 2005; Middlemas 2009). The strategic role of the SENCO is often a key element of this process, as highlighted by Svensson and Middlemas in their case study of Whistledown, a London primary school:

> Not only does the SENCO regularly involve parents in discussions about their child's provision, but she proactively empowers pupils to engage in their own learning. Through the insights offered by both pupils and parents she is then able to use the data to contribute to Whistledown's day-to-day recording and reviewing of pupil progress.
>
> (Svensson and Middlemas 2010: 142)

In terms of pupil progress, small changes made in the classroom can sometimes have a major effect on learning and teaching, and it is essential that all classroom-based staff are aware of this (such as making effective use of ICT and assistive technologies, see Judge *et al.* 2008; Lee and Templeton 2008; or Söderström and Ytterhus 2010). If learners can be encouraged to support each other in their learning activities and are working in a climate in which areas of difficulty or stress are readily acknowledged and discussed (rather than ignored or discouraged), successful inclusion will be a much more achievable goal. The Primary National Strategy underlines the importance of classroom staff actively responding to children's contributions as well as their mistakes, and indicates that the choice of language, tone of voice and manner can all play a vital role in establishing a positive ethos, in which children are able to make mistakes and take risks with their learning (DfES 2006). This is equally important for older learners, especially those who are not working to their full potential. For example, when a group of 20 first-year undergraduates (aged 18–19) were asked why they sometimes found maths and statistics difficult, the three main issues mentioned were:

> We find it embarrassing to ask for help, because we don't want people to think that we are stupid.
>
> We can't always understand some of the words used.
>
> Sometimes we can't see the whiteboard very well.
>
> (Middlemas 2011)

These are enduring issues in the inclusive classroom, and just as relevant for younger learners as for older learners, as well as for staff with responsibility for the learning and teaching environments in which they are studying. Interestingly, the issues raised by the undergraduates are virtually identical to those high-lighted in the UNESCO publication, *Embracing Diversity: Toolkit for Creating Inclusive Learning-Friendly Environments* (UNESCO 2009), which argues that learners most at risk of educational exclusion are those who are 'never asked to contribute to a lesson; who never offer to contribute; who cannot understand some of the language used; who can't see the blackboard or a textbook; who cannot hear the teacher properly; or finally, those whom no one tries to help' (UNESCO 2009: 2).

Jones explains that research originating from the disability rights movement also supports 'the need to listen to the perspectives of children in relation to developing inclusive services; services that reflect individual civil rights rather than individual needs' (Jones 2005: 60). Jones carried out research in schools to gather the views of young children in order to gain an 'insightful perspective to the inclusion debate'. Through the imaginative use of picture booklets, she gathered learners' views on a range of topics, such as *Joining In* and *Learning Together*. The subsequent data was able to provide the local Early Years Partnership team with

> insights into children's personal experiences and beliefs about the reality of inclusion. The findings from this project were disseminated to the steering committee for the Partnership in a report ... The need to continue to seek the views of children was recommended ... along with a firm reminder about the importance of addressing the issues raised by this small group of children.
>
> (Jones 2005: 65)

Listening to the student voice can be undertaken formally or informally, in a one-to-one or small group setting, by setting up a face-to-face meeting or per-haps liaising via email for older learners, by the class teacher, tutor or teaching assistant. Whichever approach is chosen, the activity invariably brings a rich set of issues for staff to consider when planning for inclusive learning and teaching environments.

Staffing and teamwork

Staffing and teamwork are key issues in the provision of effective inclusive education, both in terms of what is happening inside the classroom and outside the classroom (such as liaising with parents, attending professional develop-ment courses or taking time out to update resources or software). Salend *et al.* (1997: 7) argue that the three most important skills required by teachers working in an inclusive classroom are 'the ability to collaborate ... with other professionals', the ability to 'develop and implement strategies to accommo-date diverse learners, and the ability to develop solutions that will enhance the learning experiences of all children'. An inclusive classroom will benefit from motivated and enthusiastic staff, who are able to make use of informal networks as well as formal professional development programmes to develop their knowledge and skills base, and to be an active part of what Lave and Wenger (1991) would describe as a 'community of practice'. In the UK an example of an informal learning and support network is the *SENCO Forum*, an email list with around 1,200 members, most of whom are SENCOs or who have responsibility for students with SEN or disabilities. Day-to-day professional practice issues and queries can be aired in a supportive and informal way, and advice is readily given by teaching and academic colleagues from around the UK and beyond. For example, one member recently asked for advice about some of her students who were struggling with homework instructions at the end of a busy lesson. Wedell (2009: 55) describes the initial query:

> The problem arises when teachers give out these instructions very rapidly at the end of lessons, and pupils then have difficulty in writing them out accurately and fully. When the pupils get home, they find that they do not have all the relevant information, or that they cannot read what they have written, or both. Quite apart from the consequent anxiety, the pupils may then only produce part of what was set, or even the wrong work, and face the possibility of being given a detention. It is well known that this problem extends beyond those pupils who are actually identified as having special educational needs.

This short query raises a number of inclusive learning and teaching issues, such as the availability of professional development for staff; addressing the needs of learners in an inclusive setting; affective issues experienced by some learners; and the importance of having a good institutional policy on inclusive practice. The query was rapidly responded to, with an excellent list of workable solutions, including:

- producing homework instructions on a slip of paper, or on sticky labels, which pupils can put into their planners
- using an interactive whiteboard to display the homework instructions during the course of the lesson
- organising 'buddy' arrangements, whereby pupils who have difficulty with quick and accurate writing are matched with a mate whom they can consult if they do not understand the homework instructions
- arranging for teaching assistants to offer support as required.

(Wedell 2009: 56)

Such an informal support network offers the busy teaching team a ready supply of ideas and encouragement. The provision of advice or professional development is particularly important when staff have been appointed from non-educational backgrounds (such as school nurses, therapists or care staff). The DfES argues that a well-trained, knowledgeable staff team will be able to 'foster social and academic participation, and hence inclusion, of *all* pupils, enabling them to become more independent learners, and helping to raise standards of achievement' (DfES 2000: 9, original emphasis). Like their teaching colleagues, support and therapy staff also appreciate time away from the classroom to discuss good practice issues or to take time to learn about new developments, and this needs to be recognised by senior leadership teams. Research also suggests that one of the most fundamental aspects of the development of effective inclusive classrooms is the way in which teachers and assistants can work collaboratively, in order to meet the needs of all learners (Balshaw 2010; Florian and Linklater 2010; Liston *et al.* 2009).

Organising groups and classes

Some of the examples used in *Designing for Disabled Children and Children with Special Educational Needs* (DCSF 2009: 198) may be useful for classroom teams who wish to consider some of the issues involved when organising groups or collaborative project work in an inclusive, multi-ability class. For example, imagine that you are a member of the teaching team in this Year 3 class, which includes the following learners:

- Jenny has a physical disability, and is an able student of above average ability. She uses a wheelchair for most of the time, except when she is working with the physiotherapist, or attending her hydrotherapy sessions in the school swimming pool. Staff working in the class have just completed their manual handling training. Jenny needs to use specialist assistive software to enable her to access writing activities, as she is not able to use a pen. Some of her mobility and personal equipment is bulky, and storage of this is sometimes an issue.
- Asad has Asperger syndrome and is really good at mathematics and music, but has below-average reading comprehension. He has recently joined the school from another school in the district. When he becomes stressed or anxious in class, he knows that he can access the quiet area in the school's specialist autistic spectrum disorder (ASD) resource base.
- Jason has behavioural, emotional and social difficulties, and is currently living with his grandparents after the break-up of his parents' marriage. His attainment levels have recently fallen, but last year he was showing signs of being an above average student. He is occasionally aggressive towards other children.

(Based on ideas from the DCSF 2009: 198)

The above examples can provide a useful starting point for a learner-centred consideration of how classroom design and accommodation might be able to enhance the children's learning and teaching experiences at school. The way in which students are physically grouped in a classroom can make a considerable difference to the way in which they learn, and teaching teams might wish to consider the following issues when planning for inclusive learning and teaching:

- Which students work best in which areas of your classroom?
- How do you make decisions about what works best?
- What is the best way to arrange furniture and resources?
- How can you make more effective use of your staff team to support learning?
- Are there some minor changes that you could make which might have a major effect on the learning and social experiences of all the students in your classroom?
- Have you asked your students what they think about the groups that they are currently in?
- Where will you go for additional advice and support?

Different learners will invariably present different challenges, so it is also vitally important to bear in mind the social needs as well as the academic needs of all learners in the class when organising groups. The way in which children and young people are grouped, or not grouped, can have a major impact on the inclusive learning and teaching environment, especially in the development of social networks for learners with SEN or a disability (DfES 2007a; Koster *et al.* 2010; McLaughlin 2008). As Koster's research demonstrates, many parents see their neighbourhood's mainstream school as the ideal place for their children to develop local friendships, and a place where 'their child can build positive relationships with typically developing peers' (Koster *et al.* 2010). Koster also argues that it is much more likely for some learners (notably those with an autistic spectrum disorder or who are experiencing social, emotional or behavioural difficulties) to experience serious difficulties in forming peer relationships, whereas other children generally experience far fewer problems in this area (ibid.). Acknowledging the contribution that careful groupings can make in terms of both academic and social skills is a key issue for teaching teams in the inclusive classroom.

Other spaces to support inclusive learning and teaching

There are some children who may require additional on-site accommodation in order to make successful use of their mainstream placements (such as an autistic child, a child with cancer who has recently re-joined the school after a spell in hospital, or a child who needs to spend some time with the physiotherapist). This may be because of their underlying emotional/behavioural difficulties, or because they need 'time out' during the school day for SEN or medical reasons. There are a number of interventions which have been successfully trialled in schools in order to support such children and young people. Schools with a high number of children with behavioural, emotional or social difficulties may decide to set aside space for a nurture group. Nurture groups were originally intended for early years settings to enable young children with behavioural or social difficulties to make the transition to full-time school placements (Boxall 2002). There are now nurture groups in many primary and secondary schools, with an estimated 1,000 in operation around the UK (Rose and Bennathan 2003). In particular, some inner city areas (such as Glasgow) find them to be a particularly effective way of providing an inclusive learning and teaching environment for children and young people who have difficulties in engaging with the mainstream education system (ibid.).

A nurture group room is an integral part of the school's learning and teaching environment, but also includes the elements of a secure and supportive home. Rae (2010) explains that the room should include comfortable chairs and sofas as well as traditional classroom furniture and resources. The room should ideally have four or five distinct areas: a kitchen/food preparation area, a dining area, a role play area and a quiet area. All these areas will be appropriately resourced, while supplementary resources for different age groups will also be needed. For example, in an early years setting, a nurture group room may have:

- a writing/book making corner
- a listening station which is valuable when children want to listen to story tapes or simply record their own stories, thoughts and feelings and share them later if they so desire
- a beanbag or quiet place for children who may need time away from the rest of the group
- sand and wet play areas
- a selection of toys such as dolls, a pushchair, train sets and play bricks
- display areas for children's work
- a noticeboard for parents/carers.

(Rae 2010)

Other groups of children who sometimes experience stress or discomfort in a mainstream setting can also benefit from such a space, such as children with an autistic spectrum disorder, who may need time to be away from their classmates when they find their classrooms too noisy (perhaps during a music session) or too messy (during an art session). Research indicates that some children and young people with SEN and disabilities sometimes find school attendance very stressful or anxiety-provoking, so it is useful for schools or colleges to consider what might be done to provide suitable additional accommodation for break times or time out (DfES 2007a; Richards and Armstrong 2010). Morgan and Byer's 2008 research project indicated that a number of children and young people with SEN and disabilities reported considerable anxiety when talking about their out-of-classroom experiences:

Some said they did not like lunch and break times; they might have no friends to be with or they might get picked on in playgrounds, social areas or common rooms. The young people wanted somewhere safe to go at break and lunchtimes so that they could relax. They wanted to be with other young people 'just like me' ... Some schools and colleges have developed places for young people to go; one has developed a social garden area, another has started a gym club, or set up activities in the library. Opportunities for a quiet place, activities and for discreet support from adults when needed should be available for all young people.

(Morgan and Byers 2008: 2)

Those responsible for organising inclusive learning and teaching environments need to be sensitive to the above issues when designing their classrooms and other accommodation around the school campus, so that students with SEN and disabilities can feel safe and secure during the whole of the school day.

Conclusion

In spite of the complexity of the multi-faceted, multi-dimensional process that we call educational inclusion, and in spite of the interpretation of good practice in such widely differing ways in different contexts, I would argue that there are some key agreements emerging as to what learning and teaching in an inclusive classroom might look like. Some of the research mentioned in this chapter might be criticised as being aspirational, or too idealistic. Some of it might apply to some settings, but be unworkable in other settings. Yet I believe that the five themes identified in this chapter can strategically inform the planning process when teaching teams work towards developing effective professional practice, as outlined in Figure 6.2.

I will conclude by highlighting UNESCO's description of a truly inclusive learning and teaching environment:

A 'learning-friendly' environment is 'child-friendly' and 'teacher-friendly'. It stresses the importance of students and teachers learning together as a learning community. It places children at the centre of learning and encourages their active participation in learning. It also fulfils the needs and interests of teachers so that they want to give – and are capable of giving – children the best education possible.

(UNESCO 2005: 4)

In other words, learning and teaching activities in the inclusive classroom should be designed to be fully accessible in terms of furniture, resources, assistive technologies and specialist equipment. The classroom needs to be a place where there are regular opportunities for the student voice to be heard and acted upon. Learners should feel welcome in the classroom, as well as in other

LIVERPOOL JOHN MOORES UNIVERSITY
LEARNING SERVICES

areas of the school campus, and enjoy good relationships with school staff, who will work together with the senior management team to improve the way that inclusive provision is organised. The teaching team should develop a pro-active approach to enhancing provision for SEN and disabled students, through good teamwork, liaison, multi-disciplinary collaboration and reflective professional practice. Lastly, it is important to remember that best practice is not a static concept, but is always evolving.

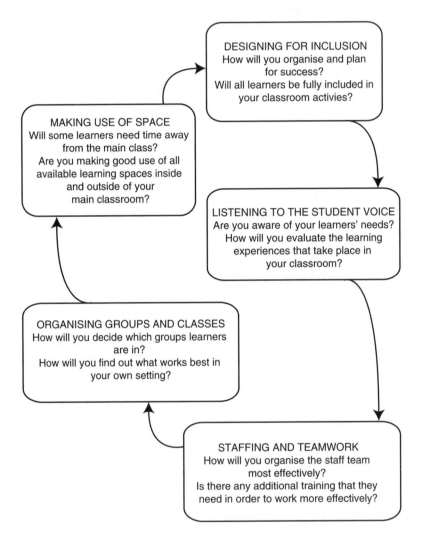

Figure 6.2 Reflecting on learning and teaching in inclusive classrooms

Chapter 7

Multi-professional working

The way forward?

Sue Soan

Introduction

It can be argued that during the first decade of this century the Labour Government embraced an inclusive and collaborative approach with regard to the provision of resources for children with special educational needs (SEN), as part of its efforts to raise standards and to facilitate social inclusion (Soan 2006: 210). One of the elements undoubtedly seen to be key to the successful implementation of this approach by the government was effective and efficient multi-professional working. This can be illustrated by their joined-up policy context through which they introduced practices such as the *Common Assessment Framework* (CAF) (DfES 2005a) and the *Lead Professional* (DfES 2005b), considering them to be the 'gelling agents' necessary to achieve multi-professional working and thus their overarching aims.

However, after several years of use in practice it has been found that these new practices have introduced additional layers of bureaucracy which professionals find difficult to implement successfully. They have also been found to be extremely time consuming and administratively heavy, with some agencies not being able to attend meetings, delaying much-needed intervention for children with SEN. These practical and impact-laden issues have therefore hindered the establishment of important multi-professional working factors, such as trust, effective communication systems and open and respectful relationships.

With the publication of the special educational needs and disability Green Paper (DfE 2011b), it appears that the Coalition Government also wishes to enable services to work together, as evidenced by their intention to implement the *Education, Health and Care Plan*, as a replacement for the statutory SEN assessment and statement for children. The Green Paper states:

> Services will work together with the family to agree a straightforward, single plan that reflects the family's ambitions for their child from early years to adulthood, which is reviewed regularly to reflect their changing needs, and is clear about who is responsible for provision ... The new 'Education, Health and Care Plan' ... will include a commitment from all parties to

provide their services, with local assessment and plan pathfinders testing the best way to achieve this.

(DfE 2011b: 16)

A significant difference expressed within the Green Paper between this and the previous system, however, is that the management responsibility for services to children and young people with SEN, including the new *Education, Health and Care Plan*, will move from central government control to local governance, with greater parental input. This suggests that the Coalition Government believes that multi-professional working will be more effective if the responsibility for its success is locally managed. They appear to have recognised the failings of a bureaucratically-led, national system that does not overtly encourage the personal ownership and responsibility of all individual stakeholders in the outcomes of a required intervention. They state:

> Frontline professionals will have the freedom to work together to develop better services for children, young people and families; and the way in which services for children and young people with SEN or who are disabled are funded will facilitate integrated and collaborative approaches by local professionals, be more transparent to parents and secure better value for money.
>
> (DfE 2011b: 93)

It is within this emerging landscape that this chapter will explore and debate the features that research and literature demonstrate enable professionals and all stakeholders to work together most effectively to facilitate an inclusive, non-deficit model of provision for children and young people with SEN (and their families). It will also examine what multi-professional working means for teacher professionalism, as core changes to teacher training education and continuing professional development are also to be introduced.

Historical overview

It was over 40 years ago that Bronfenbrenner (1970: 163) expressed his view that it was vital for an holistic approach towards provision and intervention for children and young people with SEN, requiring support from more than one agency or profession:

> It is a sobering fact that, neither in our communities nor in the nation as a whole, is there a single agency that is charged with the responsibility of assessing or improving the situation of the child in his total environment. As it stands, the needs of children are parcelled out among a hopeless confusion of agencies … no one … is concerned with the total pattern of life in the community.

Later in that decade *The Court Report* (DHSS 1976) also emphasised the importance of working with parents and with other professionals if it was in the
interests of the child. Then the *Warnock Report* was published (DES 1978).
The authors of the report stated that inter-professional working should support children with SEN by identifying, assessing, monitoring and reviewing
provision together. Thus, the 1970s saw the germination of a national 'vision'
where a more holistic, joined-up approach towards providing for children and
young people with SEN was seen to be beneficial to all stakeholders involved.

Although many benefits of joined-up working practices were envisaged for
children with SEN and their parents, it was not until The Children Act (DoH
1989) that the next important step was taken. It was this Act that made collaborative, joined-up working a local, as well as a national, issue, stating that:

> A co-ordinated approach helps to create an environment where people
> with different qualifications and experience can share skills and expertise
> and ideas in a positive way. It is important for all departments within a
> local authority to find ways of encouraging staff to work with this in mind,
> so that all the appropriate skills are available in all settings.
>
> (DoH 1989: 3, 1.16)

and

> In relation to a child who has special educational needs, the social services
> department is under a duty (section 27(4)) to help the education depart-
> ment in the provision of services, and to consult the education department
> maintaining a child's statement of special educational needs (made under
> the Education Act 1981) when placing a child at an establishment provid-
> ing education (section 28(1)). A corporate policy and clear departmental
> procedures in respect of interdepartmental collaboration will ensure good
> co-operation at all levels.
>
> (DoH 1989: 3, 1.13)

Next to reinforce the government's desire for collaborative practice for children and young people with special educational needs was the *SEN Code
of Practice* (DfE 1994). Two years after this the Education Act (1996) started
requiring schools, social services, local authorities and health agencies to share
information and help each other. Such practices were emphasised again in the
National Curriculum Inclusion Statement (QCA 1999) and the revised *SEN Code
of Practice* (DfES 2001a).

Despite the plethora of legislation and guidance promoting and supporting
multi-agency collaboration and co-ordination, evidence reported about the
effectiveness of the implementation of such practices towards the end of the
last century was poor (Dyson and Millward 1997; Pearce and Hillman 1998;
Stead *et al.* 2004). Nevertheless, despite these less positive reported outcomes,

joint working continued to be considered a vital element in enhancing practice and provision for children and young people with SEN. It was only in the first decade of this century that some research evidence concluded that there were positive outcomes of joined-up working for children, families and schools (Atkinson *et al.* 2002; Pettit 2003; Hallam *et al.* 2004 and Sloper 2004). Sloper (2004: 575) wrote:

> One model of working where evidence on outcomes for families has been reviewed is multiagency key worker systems for disabled children. Liabo *et al.* (2001) review points to some evidence of positive outcomes for families. The review concludes that while large scale, robust studies are lacking, taken together existing studies report consistent results. Compared with families who do not have a key worker, families with key workers report improved quality of life, better relationships with services, better and quicker access to services and reduced levels of stress.

However, Sloper (2004: 575) also commented that:

> Atkinson *et al.* (2002) used interviews with professionals to assess impacts on users. Whilst interviewees noted a number of impacts, such as quicker access to services, early identification and intervention, support for parents and improved educational attainment for children, no outcome data are provided other than professionals' subjective views.

It was therefore quite surprising that in 2003, 'Despite the paucity of outcome data' (Sloper 2004: 578), government policy took a radical step with the publication of the Green Paper *Every Child Matters* (DfES 2003a) outlining its intention for a whole system reform, to 'break down organisational boundaries' and to 'put children at the heart of our policies, and to organise services around their needs'(DfES 2003a: 9). Anning *et al.* (2010: 112) comment that:

> This is a holistic approach to modern childhood which underlines the importance of a comprehensive, integrated approach to professional intervention.

From the publication of this document until the end of the Labour Government's term of office in 2010, policies were published at an astonishing rate to try to ensure the successful completion of this whole system reform (DfES 2004a, 2004b, 2004d, 2004e, 2005c, 2005d).

Of significance for discussion here was the publication of *Removing Barriers to Achievement* (DfES 2004a), which highlighted the need for lead professionals and 'multi-disciplinary' teams when working with children and young people with SEN. Also in line with this and building on the Children Act 2004, *Every Child Matters: Change for Children* (DfES 2004b) provided a joined-up strategy in which multi-agency initiatives could develop. Perhaps reflecting on the research evidence, however, the government's focus, after the *Every Child Matters* agenda, shifted from considering how distinct professionals and agencies could contribute towards their desired outcome, to integrated service delivery and outcomes for children and young people and their parents. This was reinforced by the requirement for local authorities to develop *Children and Young People's Plans* by 2006 and to establish Children's Trusts by 2008. As Anning *et al.* (2010: 5) say, it was the government's intention that:

> All agencies, including health, were to share information and assessment protocols and framework. They were to plan jointly funding streams and intervention strategies.

Documents such as *The 21st Century School: A Transformation in Education* (DCSF 2008b) and *Children and Young People in Mind: The Final Report of the National CAMHS Review* (DCSF/DoH 2008) continued to reinforce the *Every Child Matters* agenda and the principle of agencies working together. Thus, it is disconcerting to acknowledge that, despite all this focus on provision and intervention, a UNICEF report in 2007 on child well-being scored the UK with the worst rates on five out of six dimensions, out of the twenty-first richest countries in the world (Anning *et al.* 2010*)*. We also know that, despite all the reforms, when it comes to life chances the gap between rich and poor is continuing to widen, and socio-economic background continues to determine a child's lifetime outcomes.

It is therefore essential that, with the publication of the *Support and Aspiration: A New Approach to Special Educational Needs and Disability* Green Paper (DfE 2011b), the opportunity is taken to reflect critically on the evidence supporting the continuation of 'working together' and of multi-professional working as a policy to achieve better outcomes for children, young people and their families. Is it that the previous policies have just required a longer time frame to embed the changes and therefore new policies need to continue on the same trajectory? Findings from reviews commissioned within the past three years with specific reference to special educational needs (Bercow 2008; Lamb 2009; Salt 2010) certainly seem to support this view, as they found that where the right support and guidance was provided quickly, specialist support services made a 'powerful difference to children's progress and their happiness in school' (DfE 2011b: 100). Or is it now time to refocus on achieving the best possible outcomes for children and young people with SEN, and less on the way professionals work together?

Definition of terminology

Here again the use of and changes in terminology has frequently led to epistemological confusion, professional mistrust between agencies in some cases and even lack of effective support for children and young people (Anning *et al.* 2010; Glenny and Roaf 2008). The importance of the use of language in aiding and cementing understanding cannot be understated and requires careful consideration as the SEN and 'joined-up' working policies are transformed. There are numerous terms used to denote 'joined-up' working – research found 52 terms as far back as 1994 (Lethard 1994). Many of these are utilised interchangeably within literature, research, policy and practice, adding to the lack of clarity and precise meaning. However, despite all the complexities involved, when viewed within the context of when they were used, each term can be seen to have evolved in conjunction with the trends and legislation presented at that specific time.

In the 1970s and 1980s language used included phrases such as 'close working relationships between professionals in different services' (DES 1978), and 'a co-ordinated approach' (DoH 1989). In the 1990s the words 'partnerships' between agencies (Frost 2005) and 'close co-operation' (DfE 1994) began to be used, and terms such as 'multi-agency', 'multi-disciplinary' and 'multi-professional' entered the discourse. The latter triad mean more than one profession, discipline or agency working with a child, but does not mean that the adults involved are working together across boundaries. In these situations a child is seen by the professionals separately, and then only vital information is shared between them.

Towards the end of the century an inter-agency or inter-disciplinary model began to emerge to represent situations where there was greater co-operation between professionals, while still working in parallel with each other. This was quickly followed by a more intertwined model, as philosophies began to emphasise the importance of seeing a child 'holistically in terms of their education and care' (Lacey 2001: 67). This model became known as 'trans-disciplinary' and 'trans-agency' working and encouraged professionals to work across disciplines to enable them to most effectively respond to a child's needs. It also highlighted the need for a 'key worker' to be identified by the team of professionals who would be responsible for co-ordinating and managing the child's and his/her family's provision (Sloper 2004; Soan 2004). This was regarded as a significant change in emphasis whereby the family and child did not have to fit around the professionals, but where the practical needs of the child and the family directed practice and provision.

As all of these models began to become utilised in practice, the new century saw the introduction of a new key concept – that of 'integration', 'integrated services' and 'integrated teams', including 'the team around the child' (Siraj-Blatchford et al. 2007). Every Child Matters documentation and the Children's Workforce Development Council (CWDC) (www.cwdcouncil.org.uk) started to use these terms when different services become one 'organisation' in order to improve services to the children.

In an attempt to clarify the use of specific terminology, Frost (2005: 13) characterised a continuum in partnership by suggesting a helpful hierarchy of terms:

- Level 1: *co-operation* – services work together towards consistent goals and complementary services, while maintaining their independence.

- Level 2: *collaboration* – services plan together and address issues of overlap, duplication and gaps in service provision towards common outcomes.
- Level 3: *co-ordination* – services work together in a planned and systematic manner towards shared and agreed goals.
- Level 4: *merger/integration* – different services *become one organisation in order to enhance service delivery*.

Looking to the future the Green Paper (DfE 2011b) uses terminology about joint working including 'working together', 'integrated services', 'integrated packages of support', 'multi–agency approach' and 'collaboration', but it suggests a different interpretation of how and by whom such work can be undertaken. It clearly states that:

> we propose to explore how professionals can work together to assess children's SEN, to plan how to provide the full range of support, and to provide parents with greater control over services for their family, including through a key worker and a personal budget.
>
> (DfE 2011b: 9)

A consistent message throughout is to provide professionals with 'greater freedom' (DfE 2011b: 102) whether through less bureaucracy, or more streamlined funding, in order to deliver more innovative models of working for children and young people with SEN. Key to this issue of joined-up working for the current government are the following factors:

- To enable professionals 'to develop innovative delivery models such as mutual, cooperatives and other types of employee-led organisations' (DfE 2011b: 102).
- To explore how the voluntary and community sector can be central to the coordination of the SEN assessment process.
- To explore the use of trained key workers from the voluntary and community sector to act as 'co–ordinators' of services for families of children with special educational needs.

The Coalition Government's *Big Society* policy is clearly impacting on the thinking behind these suggestions, but how supportive of such plans is recent research evidence?

The dynamics of multi-professional practice

Without question, the aim of any service that works with children and young people with SEN should be to achieve the best possible outcomes for them, through an effective use of resources, including professional expertise. The question to be answered here is what type of service is most effective and does it need to follow national or local systems and processes? Is multi-professional working the best model to follow? Glenny and Roaf's (2008: 121) research findings lead them to warn that:

> Collaboration was less about collaborative activity, than about communicating effectively about individual pieces of work, ensuring the patchwork of individual effort in relation to a particular family, makes sense.

Huxham and Vangen (2005: 80) advised even more strongly that 'unless potential for real collaborative advantage is clear, it is generally best, if there is a choice, to avoid collaboration'. Others such as Warmington *et al.* (2004) argue that rather than wasting resources on trying to work out what model of multi-agency work is most effective, a construct they entitled 'co-configuration' should be implemented. This model, they suggested, would allow professionals to collaborate as and when required for specific cases, at the point of need.

Conversely, there has been much research that supports collaboration and multi-professional working and integrated services (Roaf 2002; Forbes 2007; Barnes 2008).

> Multi-agency working was perceived as not only improving the accessibility of and communication between specialist professionals and services, but also providing a holistic child- and family-centred approach to supporting the child and family.
>
> (Barnes 2008: 239)

So what enables multi-professional working to be successful?

Evidence to date suggests that joint training is a significant factor. A study carried out by Barnes (2008: 238) also identified the important features of success as being:

- sufficient time, effort and resources for *regular meetings*
- accessibility of 'specialist *trained professionals* to support universal services, preferably working out of and within local schools and the community'
- *communication* by specialists with parents and professionals
- the appointment of a personal *keyworker* or co-ordinator, to share and disseminate information and to act as a *single point of contact*
- a clear and more *uniform referral approach*.

The key factor recorded in all studies consulted is an effective communication system. According to many researchers, including Glenny and Roaf (2008: 9), 'the communication system underpins everything'.

Barriers to effective multi-professional working

The barriers to effective multi-professional working include:

- different professional beliefs and practices
- professionals different pay scales and different conditions of work
- separate funding streams
- lack of joint training and CPD
- constantly changing staff
- lack of commitment to joined-up working (e.g. time, meetings, sharing responsibilities)
- too large a locality for systems to be successful.

(Mott 2004; Barnes 2008)

Professional identity and training

Research carried out by Ainslie *et al.* (2010: 31) found that there were difficulties around 'territory' and professional boundaries and that just placing professionals together did not bring about a change of working practices or a shared understanding of objectives. When considering the reasons for this it becomes obvious that such forced relationships do not have the ingredients of trust and respect which are vital factors in any effective relationship. This element of respect reinforces the need for joint training and for shared working practices to enable 'individuals *to become* not just practitioners who are subject to particular frameworks, but are active participants who critically evaluate their own practice and inform how multi-agency working and training develop' (Ainslie *et al.* 2010: 33, original emphasis).

Alongside professional values and 'culture' Ainslie *et al.* (2010) also highlighted the continuing problem of 'shared language'. They commented that:

> Where the interpretation of terms or concepts is grounded in a particular professional discourse, the development of a greater understanding of difference between professional understandings (with some reconciliation) may be more desirable and achievable than an attempt to create (or impose) a single 'shared' language.

(Ainslie *et al.* 2010: 32)

Staff stability and time

Another significant element required when considering whether to try to establish multi-agency working is staff stability. Research has found that professionals need time to overcome inflexibilities and build relationships and that short-term or ad hoc teams who meet infrequently never have the opportunity to develop effective collaborative working (Milbourne 2005; Soan 2006; Glenny and Roaf 2008; Ainslie *et al.* 2010). It has also been reported in case studies (Ainslie *et al.* 2010) that some professionals work so hard on achieving collaborative practice that this becomes the main focus for the work rather than a child's needs. At a time not only of policy change, but of the restructuring of agencies and local authorities, there is a danger that expertise, relationships and effective collaborations are weakened, if not broken, if local managers do not see the value in investing in staff stability and the necessary time to build relationships.

Funding

Separate funding streams limit the effectiveness of multi-agency working when a truly shared approach is not possible. If one agency always says it cannot contribute to a provision, then others will feel as if this partner is not committed to the work. This leads to mistrust and frustration that outcomes will not be as successful as hoped, due to the lack of commitment by all involved. The way forward here might be for multi-professional teams to apply for funding, following a thorough assessment of a child's needs from an independent body. In this way, all professionals can commit to the holistic work required without professional constraints and fear of breaking target funding limits.

Different professional pay scales and conditions of work can also cause tensions and resentment, as well as budgeting constraints and targets. Although complex and difficult, organisations are already beginning to solve this issue by constructing one single pay scale and conditions of service for all staff whatever their professional expertise.

Personal responsibility

It is also vital to acknowledge the strength and value of each individual professional when working towards a joint programme of support for a child or young person with SEN. Another important factor in the development of practice is the desire to want to engage in continual professional development. Glenny and Roaf (2008) emphasise this element for valued and valuable systems in the final paragraph of one of their books.

> The individual 'good pieces of work' need to be connected up, and this is possible, not by yet another re-organisation, but by the taking of personal responsibility and the gentle tweaking of the systems of which we are all a part. We have seen people making the system work for children.
>
> (Glenny and Roaf 2008: 124)

Conclusion

Evidence from a range of studies carried out across a couple of decades has found that professionals working together collaboratively to support and enhance the life chances of a child or young person can be instrumental in achieving positive outcomes, as long as the barriers to partnership working are limited or removed. What researchers are also saying quite clearly is that a 'one size fits all' approach to multi-professional working, through national policies, for example, will not uniformly be successful. As we have seen, professional boundaries and vulnerabilities, funding issues, strict targets and a lack of accountability can all be detrimental to effective multi-professional working. These factors can so easily become the central feature of concern for individuals when working multi-professionally and cause fractures which can fundamentally hinder the construction of the most appropriate package of support for a child or young person.

Multi-professional partnerships work, as studies can verify, when each worker, whatever their profession or involvement in the partnership, is enabled to keep the child's needs central to all discussions, where the people involved trust each other, have a common understanding of the purpose of the work and have the time needed to make well-considered plans. This approach enables everyone to accept personal responsibility for a plan's success. Processes and systems such as a 24-hour curriculum or individual education plans (Soan and The Caldecott Foundation 2010) can support the work, but it is the moral engagement of all of the partners in multi-professional working which appears to make the significant difference to the success of the programme (Glenny and Roaf 2008). I therefore believe that successful multi-professional working is not primarily about systems and processes but about a common response to need through effective communication and the sharing of professional expertise where respect for each other and belief in the same outcomes remain paramount at all times. It is also about working as well as possible with and for families with professionals recognising the individuality of each child. Nevertheless, adequate funding, respect for professional identity, sufficient time, role stability, well-managed systems and processes and joint training, as well as a well-defined, localised geographical area, are also vital elements in enabling and sustaining multi-professional working.

Research is beginning to provide a sound body of evidence regarding the factors which enable or hinder successful multi-professional working for children, families and professionals. With recent suggested policy changes advocating the implementation of many of the success criteria mentioned here, the need for further evaluation studies will be vital to ensure policy and practice does not divert from a positive pathway focused on outcome success for children and their families.

Chapter 8

Dilemmas of enablement

Inclusive and special technologies

Mike Blamires

This chapter will consider how thinking and practice has developed over the past 25 years in relation to the use of technologies to provide access and engagement with all aspects of education for learners experiencing barriers to learning and inclusion. It will relate the developments in the conceptualisation of special educational needs (SEN) to advances in our understanding of technology. This will range from the work of Mary Hope in the 1980s (special computers for special children) through the National Curriculum Access technology of Jill Day (1982), NCET's Success Maker (1986) to the classification systems employed by Chris Abbott (2006). The implications for exploiting the potential of this technology will be considered in relation to other recent findings.

The importance of technology for enabling the inclusion of learners experiencing difficulty and of disability in education

Wenger (1998) has suggested a social model of learning based upon his work with people learning in vocational settings. It has four elements that encompass many of the concerns expressed in this book about participation in learning and communities. These are: learning as meaningful experiences, learning as belonging to a group and/or institution, learning as activity and learning as becoming. The artefacts that we employ in learning can aid or hinder these processes. Technology has become ever more important in society and education, presenting teachers and learners with potentially richer environments to learn in and from. For some learners these are not just powerful catalysts for engagement and understanding, they are vital. Without them, learning and participation will not occur, or will occur only with much difficulty and effort.

Here are some examples:

- a communication aid that translates muscle movement into communication via voice or writing or converts text into a tactile representation such as Braille or spoken text.

- The use of high-quality images of real objects and people organised to aid understanding of abstract ideas or the use of symbols with speech to enable similar conceptual understandings.
- The provisionality of technology that allows interaction and risk taking, building concentration and confidence.

For some, technology in education is appealing because it can make teaching and learning easier but for others it is potentially what some think of as a fundamental game changer, although this requires a knowledge of educational technology that goes beyond superficial interactivity and communication. Perhaps we need a little magic.

25 years of special technology

In the first part of the 1980s in England, Mary Hope lead the wonderfully acronymed Special Education Micro Electronic Resource Centres (SEMERCs) funded in part by the Department of Trade and Industry but a part of the then Micro Electronics Programme (MEP) that set up 14 regional centres to promote the use of technology in schools. In the tradition of 'being special', the SEMERCs were set up later than the MEP centres and were organised as separate entities. There were four SEMERCs, each covering a quarter of England. Each SEMERC had three staff who shared the 33 local authorities in their allocation. Alongside the SEMERCs was a specialised assessment centre first based in the Ormerod special school in Oxford, Aids to Communication in Education (ACE) but also including a centre based in Manchester. These had a multi-disciplinary staff and focused upon the specialised assessment of communication needs for children whose exceptional needs might warrant this technology. The SEMERCs and ACE centres pioneered the use of email (then called BTGOLD) to share information about their activities. In order to make their task manageable, they established points of contact in each local authority, whose role was to provide local training and support for the use of technology to meet special needs. These were often based in special schools but were sometimes the local advisory teacher for special needs or information technology.

Networks of professional support

The networks became efficient due to central funding and the support from local authorities. Contacts would meet together bi-monthly at the SEMERCs to share and receive information. Crucially, for a period of five years, each SEMERC held a week-long residential workshop every summer to share and develop materials and practice. The legacy of this network is the Special Educational Needs and IT Group (SENIT) email discussion group, which is now hosted by the Department for Education.

Free software was distributed from the SEMERCs. This was at first donated software and then it was later produced by an in-house unit. The complexity of the software increased as the teachers' confidence developed. The limited nature of the software was sometimes justified in terms of user need rather than a more honest confession of lack of knowledge. The SEMERCs produced a word processor that could display eight lines of double-height letters. This worked with an external keyboard which had a matrix of touch-sensitive keys that paper overlays could be place upon (concept keyboard) while the primary MEP project produced a double-height word processor that could scroll text but at first did not work with a concept keyboard. Some teachers would plead for the need for an eight-lined word processor because they did not have confidence with scrolling word processors. At the same time, many teachers were confident enough to adapt programmes to meet their teaching needs and those of their learners with significant originality. Frequently the challenge was to make the standard software – that only expected control from a keyboard – work with an alternative input device, for example a head pointer, joystick or switch set that a child who could not use a standard keyboard was able to control.

The Magic of the Micro

Hope documented much of this innovative activity in two publications (1986, 1987). The latter was entitled *The Magic of the Micro*, a title that captured the sense of awe and excitement that many teachers had in relation to this new tool that helped them to enable the learning of children who were experiencing difficulties. Hope also made the distinction between content-bound and content-free (or framework) software, because the latter allowed the teacher to have some degree of control over the structure and content of software. This distinction and preference was not absolute as it could not be. Content-free software usually contained a range of example files to demonstrate the programme's versatility, and many teachers just used these rather than create new materials. Others used content-bound programmes such as adventure games to stimulate and deliver cross-curricular project work, perhaps supported by framework software for writing tasks.

In mainstream primary classrooms there might be only one computer and a case would have to made about access to it for learners identified as having a special educational need, unless that child had computing resources written into their statement of special needs (if their needs had been regarded as requiring such an assessment).

Hope entitled her book *The Magic of the Micro*, but it was the people rather than the technology that was magical – they squeezed a vast amount of capacity from a machine that had less memory capacity than the size of an average word processing document. The concerns were:

- Can computers be helpful for children with special needs?
- If they can, then how should they be used?
- What is the role of the teacher?

A great deal of anecdotal evidence was amassed in relation to different conceptions of SEN but little formal research was undertaken. It was clear that, for children with severe degrees of impairment or difficulty, the computer could have dramatic effects. A child with limited physical control might be able to communicate, a blind learner might be able to read and write standard text with speech synthesis and a brailler linked to a computer. But for less severe or complex degrees of disability or difficulty, the benefits were less clear cut.

Transfer and generalisation

One challenge was the classic concern of teachers: that of generalisation. Could the achievements accrued from using a computer facilitate progress away from the computer? For example, word processors were thought to be useful because the child could break out of a cycle of failure – they could write more and exploit the provisionality of the delete key and the inbuilt letter formation of the computer fonts that could print out their writing 'like in a book'. This was held to be a good outcome but teachers were expected to be sceptical. Would this success transfer to the normal classroom activity of writing with pen and paper? The potential of technology to transform the nature of work and the way we live was not accepted or fully understood so the technology had to be justified in terms of the then current technologies and habits of teaching and learning (or not). An alternative viewpoint developed which challenged traditions of classroom learning and focused on underlying conceptual development and the possibility of learning in new rather than traditional classroom ways.

The dilemma here might be posed as: how does the learner lose or gain by using technology to help their learning? They may be gaining new skills and achieving more than they have done previously but what have they lost from not mastering traditional skills alongside their peers?

An alternative perspective that was suggested at the time by Underwood and Underwwod (1990) could help in resolving this dilemma. A distinction needed to be made between authentic and inauthentic learning tasks. Forming letters by hand when word processing would be widely available would be such an example, as would be the production of graphs using ruler and pencil on graph paper. It was argued (for example Hardy 2000) that some children were failing to achieve just because of the lack of flexibility of some schools and teachers. Children had to demonstrate what they could not do rather than being encouraged to show what they could and might do. More positively, and much later, Ofsted noted this potential:

Pupils who previously were very reluctant writers have become eager authors of text for on-screen presentations of mixed images and narratives of their own experiences.

(Ofsted 2003)

The end of SEMERCs

In 1988 the SEMERCs had ended just as the National Curriculum arrived in England and Wales. Yet again the issue of difficulty and disability were an afterthought for the National Curriculum creators. Where were the programmes of work for learners whose achievements might never be at Level 1? Could the curriculum be adapted or modified for those not making the recommended progress? Bit by bit projects addressed these issues and put responses into place. The curriculum should be broad, balanced, relevant and differentiated because all pupils shared an entitlement to it. A foundation stage rather than a Level 0 was implemented to recognise the progress made by those who had previously been described as working towards Level 1.

'Differentiation' was preferred to the terms 'adaption' or 'modification' because, in the early days of the National Curriculum, there was infrequent discussion about whether or not particular aspects of the curriculum should be misapplied from some identified pupils. However, the term differentiation lived up to its name and came to mean different things to different professionals with a stake in education. At its heart was the teacher's judgement of the diversity of the pupils in the class and the amount and form of flexibility in teaching and learning that was needed for all pupils to engage with the curriculum. Such concerns could be argued as now being addressed within the area of *Assessment for Learning* (Black and William 2006) where assessment of progress is held as a central guide to future teaching and learning.

At the time of the introduction of the National Curriculum, the use of technology became focused on access, and Day (1995) suggested a way of considering these different forms that complemented the *Code of Practice on Special Educational Needs* that was developed in 1994 to ensure that schools meet their responsibilities in relation to those pupils indentified as having SEN, which then included learners with disabilities and/or medical conditions.

Access technology ... In its broadest sense, this means that IT can enable pupils to overcome the barriers to learning by providing alternative or additional methods of communicating within the learning process. It also means that IT can enable them to take advantage of their entitlement to a broad and balanced curriculum.

(Day 1995: 4)

Day (1995) suggests three forms of access:

- Physical access – 'technology at its most dramatic, liberating the pupil from the physical barriers to learning' so that a learner is provided with alternative access to communication and learning.
- Cognitive access – 'IT enables us to present the curriculum in different ways, thereby encouraging the pupil who has difficulty grasping the concepts, skills and knowledge required of him', e.g. the use of floor robots to develop spatial skills.
- Supportive access – 'the power of technology to support pupils in particular areas of difficulty', e.g. the use of the use of word processing in place of handwriting.

This classification provides a concise summary of the ways that technology might be applied, but the term 'access' has been criticised because it could be considered partial, conditional or transitory. Proponents of inclusion used this stronger term to describe the aims of educational activity with learners experiencing difficulty, disability and/or discrimination due to differences in race, ethnicity, culture or gender. Within the context of inclusion, technology could be judged in terms of its role in helping academic, physical or social inclusion. For some learners reliant on an early laptop or portable word processor, their devices enabled them to write but it made them appear different from the rest of the class. Some teachers would argue that the technology was hindering their inclusion because it made them stand out from the rest of class. What was not said was that this meant that the prejudices of other pupils were being accepted as arbiters of inclusion: in such places diversity was acceptable if it could be normalised. This could have also been an indication of the lack of confidence of staff in understanding how important technology was and how it could be utilised in lessons to support learning.

In the late 1980s the MEP had moved through a merger with NCET, a transformation into the Micro Electronic Support Unit (MESU) and then became the National Council for Educational Technology (NCET). The Special Needs and Inclusion section of NCET created a number of highly successful email forums, including the SENCO forum that survives today alongside SENIT – a resource for teachers, advisory staff and commercial suppliers to support the use of technology with learners with disabilities and/or difficulties. The latter was run on very little resources with part-time moderators ensuring that impartial advice dominates the discussion, but also that users and developers can share ideas for practice and innovation.

Integrated Learning Systems

The key emphasis in relation to NCET and special needs at this time was the implementation of what were termed Integrated Learning Systems, which were banks of networked computers utilising largely drill and practise software from the US. The intention was to demonstrate the benefits of such an approach with learners with disabilities and difficulties so that their underachievements could be remediated. Identified children were allocated time on the machines on a daily basis almost as part of a remediation programme. One of the most widely known of these systems was rather ironically called 'Success Maker'. Each system produced copious records of progress for the pupils, but Sucess Maker would allow a child to fail three times on an item and then move them up to the next level. It was neither a triumph in remedial loop creation or artificial intelligence. These systems were often administered in block time under the supervision of a teaching assistant. One could understand the dream of the government officials at the time: the application of a comparatively inexpensive technical solution to educational underachievement.

Later, under the Clinton administration, a report on the effectiveness of educational technology was commissioned and one of its conclusions was that learners from poorer social economic groups differed from more affluent learners in the kind of access they had to technology. While the report found that more progress accrued when poorer students used technology, they were given less access to it and they also tended to have access to rote learning programmes dealing with artificial problems and information rather than problems arising from the available real data.

This provides a new version of the much quoted digital divide and is an example of Dyson's (2001) Dilemma of Difference, which can be summarised thus:

> If you are judged to have different learning needs than your peers and you are provided with learning activities that are different from your peers what are you missing out on while you undertake this different provision?

The evaluations of Open Learning Systems undertaken by NCET (1986) did not appear to be concerned with that dilemma as they did not seek to answer that question.

The potential of 'real and relevant' material was noted in the DfES (2003c) report on ICT use:

> The attitudes of pupils with emotional and behavioural difficulties towards writing can be transformed by the availability of digital images to incorporate into their text.

A taxonomy of 'E-inclusion'

More recently, Abbott (2007) undertook a consideration of the use of digital technology in support of the inclusion of pupils with learning difficulties and suggested a three-component taxonomy:

I The use of technology to train or rehearse

This was technology that Abbott felt was often associated with a behaviourist model and was too prevalent and prominent and should, rather, only be used 'when needed'. Abbott was perhaps expressing a view that that rote learning and repetition were too often used with pupils identified as having difficulties or disabilities. The negative view of these programmes should be challenged because some of the programmes were highly imaginative and enjoyable in their execution and disguised their behaviourist routes very well, e.g. 'pod', a programme in which a tomato-shaped creature would undertake animated actions in response to the pupil typing in a verb, otherwise he would shake his head.

The emphasis on attainment through individualised learning on a computer, however, can be criticised in that it assumes that learning will occur in isolation with remediation or catch-up can operate without consolidation or transfer. It also assumes that skills and facts can be accumulated without contextualisation and problem solving. These assumptions can be challenged through the appropriate design and application of software and teaching activities that take advantage of the latest capacities of technology.

2 The use of technology to assist learning

Traditionally this would be associated with the use of assistive technology – technology that is used to compensate for a physical difficulty or disability and helps learning to take place but does not act as the 'key agency for learning to take place'.

3 Technology to enable learning

The use of technology that makes learning possible where it was not possible before. In this case the technology is a catalyst for learning itself.

While category 2 can be seen as vital for the inclusion of some learners in that it can include them in learning activities that they may have previously not had access to or would find very difficult, it is probably open to professional decision and negotiation whether or not certain technology applications fall into category 1 or 2. A question results but it may not be classed as a dilemma unless it is bound by organisational or curriculum constraints, which is: to what extent do different learners need to encounter 'new' material and to what extent do they need to practice and rehearse what they have already learned? The matter might be resolved by the availability of relevant, rich and meaningful data for the learners to work with.

Abbott's approach seems to assume technology used by individual learners with some intervention by teachers or learning support assistants. Ofsted reports at the time were perhaps unduly critical of teachers' use of technology, suggesting that teachers did not often know when and how to intervene in pupils' use of technology (Ofsted 2002: 16):

- Unclear objectives. ICT is used where other modes of learning would be more appropriate, or the potential of ICT applications is not fulfilled.
- Allowing work that simply reproduces information rather than enabling analysis. Often this is the result of simple copy and paste or downloads activities.
- Failure to use the full potential of particular ICT applications. For example, in mathematics, teachers do not always exploit the power of the data-handling facilities on graphical calculators or the facility of graph plotting software to transform general shapes.
- Lack of guidance for pupils. Pupils carrying out computer tasks are left unguided by adults for long periods of time.
- Too often such activities become 'independent', and lack adult intervention to support, challenge and question pupils to help them gain more understanding from the work.
- Lack of teacher intervention. In whole class teaching, the lack of appropriate intervention by teachers during the main activity of a three-part structure is sometimes a weakness. This can result in pupils working for too long at the computer without the opportunity to reflect on their work.
- Lack of recognition of pupils' expertise. Teachers often know too little about pupils' experiences of using ICT outside school. As a result, they rarely take account of such knowledge, skills and understanding in their planning or teaching.

These were criticisms that were highlighted in a report on largely mainstream use of technology to support learning so we might assume that practice in support of learners experiencing difficulty and/or disability may have been equally affected unless it was access technology which is likely to have a clear purpose that both teacher and child could agree upon perhaps.

An over-inclusive definition

If the issue was lack of guidance as to the power of the technology in enabling pedagogy, then teachers did not gain much help from the definition given in the DfES document *Towards a Unified e-Learning Strategy*, which proposed the following definition of e-learning:

> If someone is learning in a way that uses information and communication technologies (ICTs), they are using e-learning; they could be a pre-school child playing an interactive game; they could be a group of pupils collaborating on a history project with pupils in another country via the Internet;

they could be geography students watching an animated diagram of a volcanic eruption their lecturer has just downloaded; they could be a nurse taking her driving theory test online with a reading aid to help her dyslexia – *it all counts as e-learning.*

(DfES 2003c: 2, original emphasis)

The definition might be over-inclusive without identifying any criteria to evaluate learning with technology, but perhaps that is the point. Technology has become ubiquitous in education through most aspects of everyday life. We do not need to evaluate its use beyond its utility. This utilitarian or pragmatic approach to technology in education has been aggrandised by a term that aspires to be a theory – affordances. Simply put, a technological resource has affordances that a teacher or learner can exploit if they are imaginative enough to see them.

It could be argued that a vague definition alongside a focus on the superficial characteristics of technology might not help teachers to exploit the learning potential of emerging technologies. The technology is everywhere and becoming more and more versatile and accommodating. Specialised technology is becoming more mainstream and can often be customised for different needs but this important access issue should not divert us from considering how to best exploit technology to enable learning and participation. Moss *et al.* (2007) has summarised the issue as part of a DFE evaluation of the use of interactive whiteboards subject pedagogy:

> When use of the technological tools took precedence over a clear understanding of pedagogical purpose, the technology was not exploited in a way that would or could substantially enhance subject learning ... the focus on interactivity as a technical process can lead to some mundane activities being over-valued.
>
> (Moss *et al.* 2007: 9)

Over that past five years schools have invested heavily in interactive whiteboards. This has perhaps moved the focus away from what pupils can achieve with technology towards what the teacher can present to the pupils. European teachers have to be concerned with didactics but this does not appear other than as a point of criticism in UK education literature. The relation of pedagogy and didactics may need to be considered in relation to inclusion and technology.

The National College for Leadership (2005) worked with the now defunct BECTA (British Educational Communications Technology Agency, the successor to NCET, MESU and MEP) and other stakeholders to propose a model of 'e-maturity' and 'e-confidence' that outlines the characteristics of teachers, schools and learners in relation to the use of technology in schools. These include items on how to have high levels of information literacy, use ICT effectively in their own teaching, encourage children to make choices about their own use of ICT, prepare for pupils to know more than they do about ICT, build on knowledge of pupils' ICT capabilities for effective learning and use ICT effectively at a personal and professional level.

This model acknowledges the importance of knowing what the pupils know in relation to ICT and enabling pupil agency, something which has been largely absent from this consideration but that has appeared in more recent guidance. Knowledge of what is effective appears to be a given but perhaps this needs to be researched and articulated rather than be reliant upon accumulated received opinion.

Summary

This chapter has considered some of the key tensions and dilemmas underpinning the application of technology to enable the learning and participation in education of pupils experiencing difficulty and/or disability that have accrued during the development of this area. Technology has become more flexible, transparent and ubiquitous in society and has perhaps been 'taken for granted' in educational settings so that its true power to include learners has been overlooked over time. This claim needs to be tested through reference to the evidence base and new research.

Chapter 9

Inclusive and ethical research

Fiona and Graham Hallett

Introduction

Notions of 'participatory' and 'emancipatory' research have, in recent years, sought to foreground the voice of marginalised communities that so often attract research attention. While it is unsurprising that many people seek to understand the experiences of those learners at the margins, researchers new to the field might find themselves in unchartered and challenging territory. Our starting point in this chapter is to acknowledge that the ethical dilemmas inherent to researching marginalised learners are complex and demand thinking that goes beyond research guidelines, such as those advocated by the British Educational Research Association (BERA 2004), which tend to deal only with issues relating to micro-ethics such as research approval, access and confidentiality. However, we would also argue that the kind of moral and ethical dilemmas that we will discuss in this chapter are as relevant to teaching as a profession as they are to those seeking to conduct inclusive and ethical classroom research.

For example, almost 20 years ago, Sockett (1993) defined five major virtues central to the moral character of teaching professionalism: honesty, courage, care, fairness and practical wisdom, arguing more recently (Sockett 2006) that education is about the development of intellectual virtues and that teacher professionalism must be about more than functional skills and knowledge. If we relate this to classroom research, while it is tempting to devise rubrics to encourage ethical practice, such guidelines alone do little to enhance, or even define, courage or practical wisdom. What is of interest in this chapter is the extent to which teacher researchers are able to maintain a set of beliefs about the purpose of educational research within a climate of prescribed research 'standards' and whether a kind of 'values schizophrenia' (Ball 2003: 221) is experienced by individual practitioners in the process.

To return to the notion of 'teacher virtues', Sockett (2006) asserts that teacher professionalism requires the development of a number of dispositions: dispositions of character (self-knowledge, integrity – wisdom, courage, temperance, justice, persistence and trustworthiness), dispositions of intellect (fairness and impartiality, open-mindedness, truthfulness and accuracy) and dispositions of care (receptivity, relatedness and responsiveness). Likewise, Hansen (2000, 2001) in exploring teaching as a moral activity, emphasised 'the moral heart of teaching', and premised teaching as a time-honoured human endeavour to bring about human flourishing, contending that:

> The moral quality of knowledge lies not in its possession, but in how it can foster a widening consciousness and mindfulness. This moral cast of mind, embodies commitments to straightforwardness, simplicity, naiveté, open-mindedness, integrity of purpose, responsibility, and seriousness.
>
> (Hansen 2001: 59)

Classroom research does not sit beyond this moral bind; just as these premises underpin teaching, so they are at the heart of classroom research. When conducting research about any aspect of teaching and learning, integrity, open-mindedness and clarity of purpose enable us to approach classroom enquiry with a view to raising thoughtful questions about what it is that we do and why we make certain choices. Indeed, we would argue that practitioner research should, wherever possible, help us to reconnect with the moral dispositions discussed here.

With this in mind, this chapter begins with a brief analysis of the implications of the BERA guidelines for practitioners wishing to conduct inclusive and ethical research with learners, including those with additional learning/ special educational needs. From this standpoint, the chapter moves on to an exploration of how inclusive and ethical research might be realised, drawing upon case studies of typical research projects that may have been selected with this aim in mind. The chapter concludes with some consideration of how leaders of inclusion within twenty-first-century schools can strive to create 'intelligent schools' (MacGilchrist *et al.* 2004) within which all members of the school community develop morally sound enquiry-led practice which does not devolve responsibility for inclusion to a small number of key specialist staff. In such an environment, the inclusive teacher would see research as an integral part of their role – a means by which they can question their own practice in order to enhance teaching and learning for all.

In this chapter, the term 'additional learning needs' has been used to reflect a broader notion of inclusion, in line with other countries in the UK, and because the chapter is discussing ethical and inclusive research practice, which does not only apply to children with identified special educational needs (SEN).

The BERA revised ethical guidelines for educational research

The stated aim of the BERA *Revised ethical guidelines for educational research* (2004: 04) is to 'weigh up all aspects of the process of conducting educational research within any given context (from student research projects to large-scale funded projects) and to reach an ethically acceptable position in which their actions are considered justifiable and sound'.

The guidelines that follow this aim are tripartite in nature, focusing upon: responsibilities to participants, responsibilities to sponsors of research and responsibilities to the community of educational researchers. For the purposes of this chapter, we will focus on the BERA guidelines with respect to responsibilities to research participants (2004: 5–10), which include:

- dealing with issues of voluntary informed consent
- deception
- the right to withdraw
- children, vulnerable young people and vulnerable adults
- incentives
- detriment arising from participation in research
- privacy and disclosure.

While we do not deny that it is important that we deal with pragmatic matters such as consent, confidentiality and anonymity, we would contest that these issues can only be dealt with effectively when they are discussed, debated and situated within broader meta-ethical deliberations. For instance, a teacher might persuade themselves that they have not offered overt incentives to their students when conducting research without fully acknowledging the power relations that exist in any teaching and learning situation. Likewise, the existence of signed consent forms does not guarantee that the 'researched' fully understand the implications of any research to which they may have consented. In this sense, Pring (2000) makes the distinction between the *rules* and *principles* of ethics and it is of some concern to us that, when related to practitioner research, much ethical discussion can be instrumental in approach. Nevertheless, our intention in this chapter is not to dissuade practitioners from researching their practice, rather, we hope to show that ethical deliberation, whether related to research or more generally to teaching and learning, should be part of what we do as teachers and that we should embrace the uncertainty that this can involve.

In this respect, Dewey (1933, 1944) argued that means and ends are reciprocally determined, and the salient ingredient in reciprocity is the kind of practical judgement required in problematic situations that require deliberation. In response, without attempting to define the characteristics of a 'moral' or 'ethical' teacher (or practitioner researcher), our position acknowledges that professionals offer, and are expected to deliver, professional judgement as:

> an engineer without engineering judgment, a lawyer without a lawyer's judgment, or any other professional without the particular form of judgment distinguishing his or her profession from all others, would be an

incompetent 'layman' who could not honestly practice the profession in question.

(Davis 1992: 01)

In fact, it has been argued by Davis, and others, that teachers must demonstrate a disposition toward mindfulness and thoughtfulness in order to exercise professional judgement (Dottin 2009: 85). Whether mindfulness and thoughtfulness are encouraged or diminished by the BERA revised ethical guidelines for educational research is debateable.

The specific examples of classroom research that follow have been selected to enable us to make sense of what mindfulness might look like in practitioner research. These examples focus upon classroom-based research in an attempt to dispel the myth of the 'researcher' as an external research expert. Rather, the examples selected here focus upon the types of researchers who might exist in any school. We would suggest that such researchers fall into three broad categories: those who conduct research to effect some improvement in learning which may be neither inclusive nor emancipatory; those who conduct research as an aspect of a course of study, focusing on the research rules associated with their studies; and those inclusive teachers who consistently raise questions about their practice and, as a result, generate and test theories as a core feature of their daily practice. The challenge for inclusive practitioner researchers is to trust their own ethical judgement when bombarded with forms of empirical 'research' that claim to offer answers and solutions to the complexity of teaching, learning and assessment. That such research is often produced by those with a wealth of qualifications and research *expertise* belies the knowledge, understanding and capacity for practical wisdom of all members of a learning community. We hope, in this chapter, to redress this power imbalance and encourage classroom practitioners to learn to understand, and take responsibility for, their own practice through enquiry.

Let us first consider a classroom teacher wishing to engage in a piece of well-intentioned research in order to increase their understanding of the barriers to learning experienced by a learner with an identified special educational need.

Case Study I

Craig is an experienced headteacher with a mission to improve standards; the current focus of school activity is to narrow the achievement gap between expected performance scores and actual achievement for a group of Year 8 pupils in his school. Having completed a Masters' degree, Craig decides to adopt a research approach to this dilemma and designs a research intervention for the group of learners in question, all of whom are in the lowest 'set' for the core subjects. The intervention takes the form of action research, which involves withdrawing key members of the group for 40 minutes per day in order to offer intensive remedial work. Consent is given from all parents and Craig explains what he is doing, and why, to each pupil in turn. The outcomes of this intervention are written up, anonymising all pupils, and distributed around the school and local authority. As a result of the intervention, the students have all demonstrated improved attainment scores for key skills in the core subjects.

Reflection

The most obvious feature of Case Study 1 relates to the intentions of the practitioner researcher (in this instance the headteacher) which would seem to be in the best interests of his students. He is charged, as a school leader, with ensuring that *all* learners are enabled to achieve the highest standards possible (whether or not we agree with nationally prescribed attainment levels, as the primary driver for an education system is beyond the scope of this chapter). As such, he has decided upon a withdrawal intervention and has invested energy into ensuring that the pupils, and their parents, are informed about his intentions and that the parents are given the opportunity to withdraw consent. In this way, Craig could be seen to be conforming with the BERA guidelines that relate to deception, privacy and, to some extent, right to withdraw. In addition, Craig has not offered obvious incentives to the pupils who participated in the intervention in the form of direct rewards (such as stickers, certificates or treats). Nevertheless, if we return to the teacher virtues advocated by Sockett (1993, 2006), we might be inclined to think a little deeper about the BERA guidelines that relate to voluntary informed consent and might view the notion of 'right to withdraw' from a different perspective. Indeed, a thoughtful practitioner researcher might question how far learners in compulsory education can ever withdraw from a research intervention and whether, in this situation, parental consent is anything more than a superficial formality. For example, very few parents might have the courage to refuse consent for an educational intervention where the intention is to enhance core subject knowledge, even if they believed that withdrawing their child from their peers every day did little for their child's self-esteem.

Sockett's teacher virtues also enable us to engage thoughtfully with the idea that detriment can arise from participation in research even when the research itself is well intentioned. If we pay attention to the terms used by Sockett when describing the dispositions that lead to teacher virtues, such as justice, courage, open-mindedness and relatedness, we might be inclined to question why an approach that segregates learners from their peers is a common intervention of choice. Moreover, if we were to select open-mindedness and justice as the drivers for practitioner research we quickly realise that the ethical researcher would spend a considerable amount of time analysing the ethical probity of their research intervention prior to thinking about consent and privacy. Such practitioner researchers might then question why intervention practices in their school or setting have evolved as they have; this is the challenge and the benefit of really thoughtful practitioner research.

It takes courage to question the automatic use of withdrawal or, to cite another common intervention practice, individual support from teaching assistants, but if we are to genuinely develop our practice beyond historically defined ways of working, courage is a necessary feature of our research armoury.

At this point, it is worth reflecting upon how an ethical practitioner (or researcher) would address the dilemma facing Craig. A teacher determined to behave in an open-minded way focusing on justice, fairness and relatedness might design an action research project in co-operation with learners and their parents. Furthermore, if the aims of this project were to raise attainment without excluding any learners from the social setting of their classroom, a range of exciting and innovative ideas might emerge. The most important outcome of such an activity, however, would be that members of the school community would be encouraged to question their practice.

It may be, as a result of this debate, that parents and pupils decide to create interventions over which they have ownership, rather than seeing the teaching staff as the only members of the school community able to impact upon learning. Collective action of this nature, often described as a feature of an 'intelligent school' (MacGilchrist *et al.* 2004), certainly challenges the status quo and, we would argue, enables practitioner research to become a vehicle by which power relations are levelled across a school community. It could also be argued that practitioner research of as this nature could pave the way for more ethical teaching and learning practices across a school and change the focus of school-based research from one that attempts solely to solve problems to one that aims to explore important pedagogical questions. Finally, research of this nature will, quite rightly, challenge the idea that responsibility for 'improving' learning for 'hard to reach' pupils or those with additional learning/special educational needs rests with the expert outside the classroom, and not with the practitioner.

Case Study 2

Patricia is in her second year of teaching and in the first term of a Masters' degree. As part of her MA she is required to conduct an educational enquiry and decides to use this as an opportunity to analyse the life-world of a child with Autistic Spectrum Disorder (ASD) in her Year 6 class. Having read the BERA revised ethical guidelines for educational research she designs a case study that draws upon the oral histories of the learner and his parents. As the learner experiences difficulties understanding abstract concepts such as 'research', the parents give consent on his behalf explaining to him that 'Miss wants to get to know us better'. The research progresses well until the parents disclose negative experiences with other teachers in the school in response to a research question that Patricia had designed around helpful and unhelpful pedagogy. The parents, having voiced their concern, have approached the headteacher with a view to enquiring why no other member of school staff had shown interest in their experiences, and to complain about the staff members that they felt had previously marginalised their child. As one parent commented 'it was only when we said it out loud that we realised that we shouldn't be putting up with this'.

Reflection

This is a complex situation that raises questions about first, the nature, extent and quality of informed consent, linked to notions of capability; second, the exercise of the 'teacher virtues' alluded to earlier; and third, further developing the point raised in Case Study 1 about whole school responses to pupil and parent voice, and the degree of empowerment that can easily be the consequence of such open communication.

It is worth noting that, in terms of professional and practical judgement (Davis 1992; Dottin 2009) and the mindfulness and thoughtfulness that such judgement demands, it could be argued that adopting a thoughtful approach to research is the primary means by which an ethical teacher can engage with practitioner research. A thoughtful approach should involve a thorough and careful review of the potential impact of the research prior to any attempt to embark on the project. We would argue that a major area for consideration at this stage concerns consent in general, and notions of *informed* consent in particular. In revisiting these notions, it is worth asking: what would an ethical practitioner researcher do?

In relation to informed consent, Patricia has gained proxy consent via the learner's parents as she has rationalised that the pupil would not understand her intentions in terms of researching his life-world. It would be our initial contention that this rationalisation is based on a false ethical premise, in that research cannot be seen as truly ethical if the consent of the research subject is not sought and obtained. If the latter is not possible, it would seem that practitioner research of this nature, designed for small-scale interventions of important, if limited, ambition, should not be continued.

The major danger inherent in the practice of gaining informed consent lies in the nature of qualitative difference. In Case Study 2, at what point can the pupil be judged to be unable to give consent to the request to research? It becomes all too easy to deny pupils in certain categories the right to make these decisions, almost by the default position of having been labelled. That this leads to a hierarchy of 'labels' further complicates the position, for example should a researcher consider a pupil with a specific learning difficulty more able to consent than a pupil with Attention Deficit Hyperactivity Disorder, who would be more able than the pupil with ASD cited in Case Study 2, and so on. Indeed, it would almost seem that this sort of hierarchy is inherent in the BERA guidelines, where 'vulnerable children' and 'vulnerable adults' are seen to be in some important way in a different category to 'children'.

It might be more useful to consider a capability approach to this dilemma. In this situation, all pupils would be considered capable of giving informed consent, to a greater or lesser degree, and it is this that needs exploring and understanding in our quest to ensure that informed consent exists. That this is potentially difficult cannot be denied – reaching and hearing the voice of a pupil with limited communication, for example, will be time consuming and will require ingenuity and innovative thinking. However, for an ethical practitioner such steps seem a necessary way forward, and infinitely preferable to an approach that simply dismisses this voice in preference for the easily obtained permission of a parent. It may be that an understanding cannot be achieved; it is here that we would argue that our second point, regarding 'teacher virtues' becomes relevant.

If a potential researcher is employing dispositions of character, intellect and care (Sockett 1993, 2006) then decisions about informed consent cannot be divorced from other judgements made about the ethical nature of the project. It may be, as suggested earlier, that an understanding cannot be reached. In this case, it would be argued that the research should not go ahead, even where a proxy voice could be sought. This seems to be as much a part of the moral framework of the decision-making process as not continuing with a project when the information elicited is likely to be problematic for both participants, and for those named in the research. Similarly, a question of degree about consent might arise, and this again seems to require the exercise of ethical professional judgement on the part of the researcher, with a presumption of always erring on the side of caution. In this case, having sought consent from the pupil, the researcher may decide that the test of informed consent has not been met, and this precludes the research in this form. This would not prevent a research focus on the parental life-world in relation to their experiences in advocating for their child, and this would be an area where informed consent will be easy to obtain.

That this might well lead to further difficulties is immediately obvious, and this leads us to our second consideration, regarding the exercise of 'teacher virtues'. A research process of this type cannot simply be confined to questions, answers, recollections and reflections that conform to the researcher's ideas of relevance and usefulness. In giving the opportunity for the voice of a pupil, or in this case, the parents of a pupil, to be heard, we may well become party to information or opinions that are critical of the setting in which we work. Indeed, given the reported experiences of parents of pupils with SEN and/or disability in their dealing with professional expertise (for example Pinkus 2005) it would seem to be likely that these frustrations will inevitably surface. Where the criticisms and concerns are directed at those who work in the particular setting under consideration, it would seem that a burden falls on the researcher to proceed with integrity and absolute discretion, to ensure that no leakage of information can be ascribed to a lack of mindfulness and thoughtfulness in their professional judgement.

If a potential conflict arose consequent on the careless release of information from the researcher – remembering the closeness of relationships in the average staffroom – great damage could be done, falling outside the more narrowly defined detriment inherent in the BERA guidelines, which only seem to protect the research subject. Of course, in the case study under consideration, it is likely that any public criticism of other professionals, whether arising from comments from a pupil, or from newly empowered parents, will cause detriment to the research participant, who is likely to be easily identifiable as the only ASD pupil in the school, even where anonymity has been guaranteed. In this scenario, the notion of informed consent also becomes irrelevant; if the researcher has acted with propriety, and has kept all information totally confidential, it would seem inevitable that a decision would have to be taken to restrict publication of research outcomes, to provide the degree of confidentiality that an agreement to anonymise seems to warrant.

Of course, a researcher acting within the professional protocol outlined above would surely have informed the parents and the pupil concerned that the questioning process might be upsetting and that emergent information would normally be shared with both the wider school community and potentially the world beyond the school, where matters of broader interest are revealed. In doing this, the practitioner researcher is informing participants of potential detriment rather than simply informing them of her motivation for conducting the research. Had Patricia had a conversation of this nature with the learner and his parents, they may have decided together how they would respond to potential difficulties and who they would share the research with. Agreeing such a protocol prior to conducting research offers a measure of emotional protection to all involved and changes informed consent from a research *rule* to a research *principle* (Pring 2000). Ultimately, even in this situation, we would assert that the most ethical response is likely to be to only release material that continues to safeguard the child concerned.

We would also acknowledge, in considering our third point, about empowerment, that by releasing the voice of participants, the researcher has to assume a further burden. In the short term there will be a need to demonstrate empathy and responsiveness to the newly awakened and expressed feelings of both the learner (who is the research subject) and perhaps more particularly the parents, who may be feeling grave concerns about the efficacy of their efforts to best obtain parity and inclusion for their son. In the longer term, the researcher might also need to reflect on the potential for the further actions that this form of empowerment might give to the parents, in acting on their newly found agency. While the practitioner can act in a way that is wholly consonant with guidelines such as those promulgated by BERA, in withholding research data that is damaging or detrimental to the subject, this certainty cannot be extended to the parents. If they wish to pursue issues that they feel empowered about as a result of finding their voice, that is clearly their right, but it is also their responsibility.

Case Study 3

Susan is an experienced teacher who regards her practice in Year 3 as fully inclusive. In developing her classroom ethos, Susan focuses on the individual needs of each pupil and builds a personalised learning programme for each. This fits within a curriculum framework that is creative, thematic and child centred; she eschews ability groups, withdrawal programmes and rigidly formulated lesson structure. She uses assessment for learning to drive achievement forward. In this sense, she uses action research processes to shape all work in her class. She describes herself as an exponent of research-led practice.

Reflection

What does research-led practice mean in this case study? It could mean that this is a continuous process operating at the whole class and individual pupil level, where emerging practice rests, as a continuous assessment of individual and class needs. There is no set starting point for this research because it occurs as a naturalistic part of Susan's pedagogy. Formal research consent is not sought, although a generalised permission to work in this way is sought from parents and pupils at the beginning of the school year. However, in this way, practice represents the BERA guidelines in a strict sense, and the dispositions alluded to by Sockett and Dottin earlier in this chapter. The difficulty will occur if Susan is asked to disseminate or demonstrate her practice to a wider audience, as there will be no delimited research process on which to make judgements.

In view of this, and to return to the points made in the introduction to this chapter, the practice described here goes beyond being a 'researcher' and encapsulates what it is to be an inclusive and ethical teacher within a community of practice that values genuine participation. Indeed, this teaching and learning climate enables inclusive and ethical research to be born of the virtues embedded in everyday practice and it would be difficult to imagine that any learner, including those with additional learning/special educational needs, would be marginalised by either the practice or by any research intervention that might evolve from the teaching and learning described here.

Nevertheless, practice of this nature cannot exist in a vacuum and must be nurtured by a wider school community that renders emancipation of certain learners unnecessary due to a commitment to democratic engagement with teaching, learning and research across the whole school. Susan is enabled to develop inclusive and ethical research-led practice because she is a member of a community of teaching and learning that nurtures the virtues and values discussed throughout this chapter. If she were required to disseminate or demonstrate the research that informs her teaching, it would be easy for her to reflect upon the ethical commitments that must guide her as she will, inevitably, be exploring such issues on a daily basis.

Conclusion

As the case studies analysed here typify the forms of research practice that characterise twenty-first-century classrooms, we would contest that all educational practitioners have the capacity to become inclusive and ethical educational researchers. The realisation that the moral and ethical issues that are raised by research are central to teaching and learning should provide an incentive for all members of a school community to base their practice on thoughtful enquiry. Educational leaders and those with designated responsibility for inclusion and SEN have a crucial role to play in this endeavour – to empower the voice and reflective capacity of all members of the school community. In this sense, we would encourage leaders of twenty-first-century schools to see and nurture the capacity around them rather than seek to impose their own truth on the practice of others. This is no mean feat and takes wisdom, courage, impartiality and receptivity (Sockett 2006), however, such virtues should not be limited to classroom practice but should provide the basis for our school-based research endeavours, and lead to school development characterised by emancipatory, empowering and ethical research-led practice.

Chapter 10

Developing inclusive schools

An international case study

Peter Grimes

Introduction

Through a case study from Lao PDR (People's Democratic Republic), this chapter reflects on the inclusive development of schools internationally, focusing on the ways in which teachers develop their understanding of inclusion. It is concerned with the development of more inclusive practices and systems in international contexts, particularly those which might be considered as especially challenging, both socially and economically. The chapter also views policy changes through the lens of practice development at local level in schools and communities, with the challenges faced in trying to ensure that inclusive values are at the heart of school development.

Internationally, the term inclusive education (IE) is usually used to describe projects or initiatives which are fundamentally concerned with ensuring that disabled children are attending school; although inclusion has come to signify a broader notion which focuses on a values-based approach to education and removing barriers for all young people. It is argued that inclusive values such as equality, rights and participation need to be clearly related to action in order to ensure that barriers to participation and achievement are removed and schools and systems are reformed to enable all students and communities to be valued equally. The development of schools internationally should also be seen against the back drop of *Education for All* (EFA) (UNESCO 2008) and the EFA fast track initiative (Buse 2005; World Bank 2008). It is increasingly recognised that an inclusive approach to the development of educational strategy is required if the *Education for All/Millennium Development Goals* (EFA/MDG) (United Nations 2008) are to be achieved in a meaningful way, ensuring equitable experiences for all students.

Recent international research provides evidence that the professional development of teachers is a key factor in ensuring that inclusive education policy does not become 'empty rhetoric' (Wrigley 2011). Case studies which indicate the importance of professional development from a range of international settings include South Africa (Ntombela 2011), China (Song 2010), Mexico (Cedillo and Fletcher 2010), Vietnam, Laos and Cambodia (Grimes *et al.* 2010) and Australia (Deppeler 2010). This chapter will focus on research findings which relate to the development of teacher identity at local level and the tensions involved in trying to apply concepts which have been generated through western theories to schools and teachers in south east Asian contexts. The term 'contexts' is used because assumptions can be made that there is a singular culture or context applicable to a region or country although research indicates that this is not a useful way of conceptualising teacher identity, which is dependent on local cultural factors and influences.

Methodology

The data presented draws on three different research projects within Lao PDR undertaken between 2004 and 2009. One of these was concerned with the evaluation of the Lao PDR Inclusive Education Project between 2008 and 2009 (Grimes 2009). The second set of data draws on case study research and the third is derived from data collected through a three-year school self-evaluation/collaborative action research project undertaken with nine schools in the IE Project between 2004 and 2007, the *Improving Quality Schools For All Project* (Grimes *et al.* 2009a).

My position in writing this chapter is problematic in that I combine the roles of researcher, project consultant and project evaluator. As project consultant, I had the advantage of being closely involved in the project's development from 2003 to 2009, and led the team which conducted the final evaluation of the project. Between 2005 and 2009 I was also collecting data from one case study school in the project as part of my PhD research. These interlinked roles enabled me to make connections between different aspects of the project and to present a more detailed picture of the achievements and challenges faced. The disadvantage of my position is that I may, at times, have been too close to the work to be able to maintain objectivity and criticality. This is a challenge faced by participant researchers in many contexts (Altrichter *et al.* 2007; Ely *et al.* 1991; Sherman and Webb 1988).

Education in Lao PDR

The Lao education system is grade-based with a primary national curriculum which relies on set textbooks. Children begin primary school in Grade 1, at the age of seven and complete at the end of Grade 5, when they are 11. A small proportion of children attend pre-school and a similar number go on to secondary school. The country currently has 867 pre-schools, 8,529 primary schools and 926 secondary schools. The teaching language medium is the Lao language, but many children have a different first language, making them vulnerable to experiencing language- and understanding-based barriers to participation and achievement in school. These children are less likely to attend school and more likely to drop out of school (Save the Children 2008).

There are approximately 40,000 teachers, many of whom have received only one year of basic training, although the current national strategy is to 'upgrade' teachers through in-service training and improving initial teacher training. The Ministry of Education in Lao PDR is publically committed to reaching its *Education For All* targets (UNESCO 2008), although it is acknowledged that there are serious challenges in achieving these by 2015 (Ministry of Education 2008).

The Lao PDR inclusive education project

This project was one of the longest running projects of its kind internationally, from May 1993 to 2009, when external funding came to an end. The project has been described in a book published by Save the Children in Norway (Grimes 2009).

Before the establishment in 1992 of a special school for blind and deaf children, in the capital city of Vientiane, Lao had no education provision for disabled children. The *Inclusive Education Project* (then known as the *Integrated Education Project*) was introduced in the 1993/4 academic year to address this issue, and was seen as a significant step towards fulfilling the *Convention on the Rights of the Child* (UN 1989), as well as the *United Nations World Programme of Action Concerning Disabled Persons* (UN 1982). With support from UNESCO and Save the Children UK, the project had expanded by 1995–6 to include nine primary schools and three pre-schools. Each year, with the Swedish International Development Cooperation Agency (SIDA) becoming the major donor, the project expanded to include new schools, provinces and districts. There were three phases of the project's development:

- Phase 1: 1995–1999, 80 schools (in total).
- Phase 2: 2000–2004, 369 schools (in total).
- Phase 3: 2005–2008, 539 schools (in total).

The 539 schools included pre-school, primary and secondary, three special schools and covered all 141 districts, in each of the 17 provinces throughout the country. By 2008, it was estimated that over 3,000 disabled children were being educated alongside their peers.

The aim of the project was to ensure that disabled students had access to school and experienced 'meaningful, relevant and quality learning' (Holdsworth 2003). In 1993 pedagogy was based on traditional approaches involving high levels of rote learning and copying from the blackboard. The project focused on training and supporting teachers to improve the quality of education by introducing child-centred approaches to learning, involving:

- a range of different activities to take place during the lesson
- increased use of resources

- a range of approaches to student groupings
- different questioning styles
- the development of lessons which had relevance to real life or learners' own experiences.

This approach became known as the *IE 5 Point Star* and diagrams of the five points, in a star shape, were displayed in schools which received training. The thinking behind this was based on the Salamanca Statement:

> The challenge confronting the inclusive school is that of developing a child-centred pedagogy capable of successfully educating all children, including those who have serious disadvantages and disabilities.
>
> (UNESCO 1994: 6)

The twin-track approach (Miles and Singal 2010) of trying to ensure quality provision for disabled children at the same time as introducing new teaching approaches was challenging and problematic. The Ministry of Education in Lao PDR and Save the Children UK believed from the inception of the project in 1993 that system reform would take time, and children with visual and hearing impairments would need specialised support to enable immediate access to education. This took the form of segregated provision in special schools. Children with hearing loss who needed sign language were taught separately throughout their school career. Children with loss of vision were taught Braille in special schools and then introduced into mainstream schools where the staff had been given additional training in Braille. The project only attempted to enrol children whose needs were described as 'mild to moderate'. Although attempting to break away from a medical model, this language was indicative of it, not least in the lack of clarity of definition. It also left unanswered the question of what happened to those whose needs were deemed more serious and were thus unable to attend either special or mainstream school.

As the project grew in terms of the number of schools and children it catered for, the team managing the project evolved a broader understanding of the term 'inclusive education', reflecting the way in which inclusion became a subject of debate internationally (Peters 2003). Slee's argument that inclusion as a concept became confused and lost its clarity, meaning different things to different people (Slee 2004) has been supported by many writers in the field (Ainscow 2005b; Howes *et al.* 2009a). For some, inclusion is viewed as an attempt to move away from segregated provision for disabled students towards creating mainstream placements for them (Rieser and Mason 1992). For others it is a broader concept concerned with identifying and removing barriers to participation and achievement for all students (Booth and Ainscow 2002), therefore maximising the participation of all in mainstream schools (Allan 2003) and demanding radical changes within schools (Barton 1997). In response to this, the name of the project changed from the '*Integrated*' to

'*Inclusive' Education Project*, as it evolved into a project which, although still viewing the rights of learners with disabilities to have equal access to mainstream education as fundamental, also focused on the importance of ensuring that all students were experiencing a 'quality' education (UNESCO 1994: 6) by fully participating and achieving in school.

The term 'quality', as with inclusion, is often rather loosely defined (Sayed 1997) with important parallels between the concepts of 'inclusion' and 'quality education'. Sayed and others (Bunting 1993; Holt 2000) argue that definitions of quality are driven by the values and beliefs which underpin education. Concepts of quality education have been partly shaped by the way that the international educational community has sought to measure it. It has been argued that 'an "economist" view of education uses quantitative measurable outputs as a measure of quality, for example enrolment ratios and retention rates ... and cognitive achievement as measured in national or international tests' (Barrett *et al.* 2006: 2). I would argue that this is an approach which has become overriding within a policy setting which is effectively dominated by *Education for All* (UNESCO 2008) and the EFA fast track initiative (Buse 2005; World Bank 2008). The measurement of the quality of the educational outcomes for children attending schools in the *IE Project* in Lao PDR can be viewed in this way. This can also create a smoke screen that covers the true story beneath the statistics (Grimes *et al.* 2009b). Understanding the reality of life in schools involves engagement with culture and community at a local level, which means abandoning concepts which limit our understanding to national cultural stereotypes or reliance on national data sets.

Concepts such as 'child centred', 'child friendly' and 'active learning' have begun to permeate school development initiatives in much of south east Asia and particularly in Lao PDR. The Salamanca Statement refers to inclusive schools 'developing a child-centred pedagogy' (UNESCO 1994: 6). Child-centred education is a construct emerging from the Vygotskyian theory of child development (Vygotsky 1987) where children learn through activity. Sriprakash, in a recent discussion of approaches to child-centred education in rural Indian primary schools, describes a child-centred classroom:

> Learners might have considerable control over the use of time, space and resources in the classroom, which positions them as self-regulating, and constructs the teacher as a facilitator.
>
> (Sriprakash 2010: 298)

In south east Asia, the concept of 'child centred' is closely linked to the development of UNICEF's 'child friendly' schools. In a 1997 lecture, Hammarbeg linked child-centred education to the Salamanca Statement and described schools which might be enacting this philosophy as 'child friendly' (Hammarbeg 1997: 19). Child friendly was also linked to child rights, and in such schools

The child has the right to be curious, to ask questions and receive answers, to argue and disagree, to test and make mistakes, to know and not know, to create and be spontaneous, to be recognised and respected. There should be recognition in school of the reality that pupils are individuals and learn in different ways and at a different pace. A child-centred school gives the teacher a new role: less of a lecturer or a classroom police officer, more of a facilitator or group leader. A modern teacher will organise activities, provide materials, stimulate, guide and give advice. The pupils should have opportunities to 'learn how to learn' as a basis for continued, lifelong learning.

(Hammarbeg 1997: 19)

The UNICEF model of child-friendly schools (Shaeffer 1999) developed these ideas to create a framework for child-friendly environments, which, it was argued, schools should be aiming to create. The UNICEF framework presents the child-friendly school as one which

recognises, encourages and supports children's growing capacities as learners by providing a school culture, teaching behaviours and curriculum content that are focused on learning and the learner.

(Shaeffer 1999)

In Lao PDR, this framework has become the model for all schools in the country. The new *Education Sector Development Framework* (Ministry of Education 2009) has attempted to bring together all the different educational initiatives under one umbrella, aiming to support the country in reaching its EFA targets and making every school a 'child-friendly school'. Such development agendas are often driven by multilateral agencies such as UNICEF, UNESCO and the World Bank (King 2007), perhaps without critically exploring the complex processes which enable changes in practice to develop sustainably, and strong ownership of the process by developing countries is not always apparent. Nguyen *et al.* make the point that in contexts such as south east Asia, the pressure exerted by international agendas to reform education systems as quickly as possible, runs 'the risk of "false universalism" involving the relatively uncritical adoption of various western approaches' (Nguyen *et al.* 2009: 109).

Teachers' actions and responses at a local level

After the initial pilot phase of the *Inclusive Education Project* it was acknowledged that training was not necessarily the answer to developing teachers' practice. There was clear evidence from the first two years that

inexperienced teachers had been asked to do things that were too difficult for them at that time and with their current level of skill. They needed less theory and 'training' and more 'support' in a situation where the difficulty they faced was controlled and would not overwhelm them.

(Holdsworth 2003: 16)

A support structure was developed with local advisors trained to work with schools. Implicit in the policy framework being developed by the project was that, in order to develop more inclusive practice, there was a need for teachers to undergo a pedagogical shift – away from teacher-centred practices, seen as old-fashioned and traditional, and towards child-centred practices, identified as inclusive and child friendly. The training to support this shift in pedagogy was initially based around a five-day course that was attended by all the teachers in the case study school. The school would then be supported by two-to-four visits a year from the local advisor, trained in the same way as the teachers but with more emphasis on management of the project in their district.

My initial observations of practice in the school in 2004, confirmed by interviews with the teachers, led me to realise that the teachers were still struggling to change their pedagogy. They were able to identify changes in practice related to their training – such as the use of resources and simple questioning techniques to check children's understanding – but they were aware that more was expected from them than they were able to deliver. One example was group work, encouraged by the Ministry of Education in terms of discussion and engagement with lesson content. Advisors had been trained accordingly and were passing this new approach on to schools. The teachers in the case study school explained:

> We know it's a new idea and seems like it could be helpful because the children can talk to each other. But we don't really understand it properly.

When asked how the local pedagogical advisor was supporting them and what kind of advice they were receiving, the teachers said that they had simply been told to put the children into groups for 20 minutes in the middle of each lesson. Their impression was that the local advisor did not really understand the principles of the approach either, which was confirmed when I later interviewed the local advisors. This pattern was repeated in other schools. On one level this appears to be a case of the importation of pedagogy proving to be problematic because of awareness of the need to develop the recipients' understanding of how the new practice should work. However, as has been argued by researchers working in the field of comparative education (Crossley and Vulliamy 1998; Nguyen et al. 2009: 113), it is problematic often because of a lack of awareness of culture and context which can create their own barriers to effective transfer.

Several years of field work in Lao enabled me to develop a deeper understanding of the cultural factors which impact upon the enactment of policy into practice. Teachers may not have the 'cultural space' that policy takes for granted in which to develop their practice. Based on Stephens' work (2007: 203–212) and my field experiences, I developed a mind map of the interlinking cultural factors and constraints/possible facilitators affecting teacher development (Howes *et al.* 2009b). Factors identified as constraining the development of reflective practitioners included political, social and religious factors. So, for example, Buddhism in Lao PDR encourages believers to attain a state of no self, where the issues of day-to-day life become irrelevant to the spiritual development of the individual. This may conflict with the development of a professional dialogue which aims to encourage an awareness of the 'self' in a school and social context. Lao PDR has a social structure, headed by a one-party government which is essentially centralist, authoritarian and hierarchical, reflecting both the communist political ideology of the government and deep-rooted Confucian influences on Lao society (Stuart-Fox 1997). The outcome of these factors is often deference to authority, with any forms of support being interpreted as a covert form of monitoring and control. These constraints appeared to affect the development of reflective dialogue with or between teachers.

My initial experience of working with the teachers at the case study school was that, while they were very welcoming of me and appeared enthusiastic about engaging with my research, I had to be wary about the reliability of their responses. For example, I gave all the teachers an initial exploratory questionnaire before I began researching in the school. My aim was to encourage the teachers to think about their own views of the school, what it was trying to achieve and how this related to the notion of being an 'inclusive school'. I met with the teachers and talked through the questionnaire, explaining that I would like them to fill the questions in on their own, not to work together, so that they could say what they really thought. I had discussed this with the principal beforehand and she carefully reinforced the message that the teachers needed to be honest and explain their own opinions. The outcome was five identical questionnaires, with the same answers, word for word. I asked the teachers if they had worked together or had been in the same room when they filled it in. 'No, we all filled it in at home, like you told us to', was the group response. An important lesson had been learnt and one which also provides a window through which to begin understanding the complexities involved in expecting teachers to think and speak more openly.

It can be too easy to interpret Asian cultures as being mostly associated with collectivism, meaning there is an overarching sense of responsibility or duty to the group or state but there is a strong impression of collectivism in the above example. Nguyen *et al.* (2009) explore this in their discussion of co-operative learning in Asia. and identify the importance of conceptualising trust and identity in trying to make sense of the way in which individuals in Asian contexts engage with new developments and initiatives. One interpretation, then, could be that the teachers' responses to the questionnaire was a retreat into a collective position which felt safer and non-threatening, partly because I was not yet a trusted member of the group but also because I represented a set of values which were not completely in line with those of the group. This seems a significant piece of learning for me as a researcher trying to understand the ways in which the role of the 'other' – whether researcher or consultant – supported the development of more inclusive practices.

The role of the 'other', the sensitive outsider who can support and challenge as a critical friend, is well documented in western literature on the development of inclusive schools (Booth and Ainscow 2002; Howes *et al.* 2009a; MacBeath 2006). It has also been noted that in research projects of this kind, where a western outsider enters a culturally different context, it is often challenging for the researcher to access the research problem and that 'insider credibility' can help to overcome this (Chawla-Duggan 2007). The teachers at the case study school identified the significance of their learning conversations with other teachers and myself as their critical friend as being crucial to their changes in practice. My approach built on Hanko's work in asking teachers a series of 'answerable questions' (Hanko 1999) which focused them on different areas of practice, encouraging professional reflection and analysis without providing negative or positive judgements.

I found, over time, that space for the development of professional dialogue was created, often because of unexpected factors. One such factor was collaboration with other schools through the *Improving Quality Schools for All Project* (IQSA), aimed at developing more inclusive practice in the school, based on self-evaluation processes and driven by a set of inclusive values in the form of indicators (Booth and Ainscow 2002; Grimes *et al.* 2007). Teachers appeared to be learning in this context because they were driving the agenda for change and development. Schools were supported by a team of advisors who were learning about the process in collaboration with the teachers. There was a sense of ownership among the teachers, and the concept of 'active learning', which they had been trying to develop in classrooms, was enacted in their workshop sessions and in their work in school.

Self-evaluation and other mechanisms of accountability are part of a global agenda which has been pushed by external multilateral agencies, and so it is questionable how much ownership a country such as Lao PDR takes in such initiatives (King 2007: 377), but this research indicated that such initiatives can have *locally* created a greater space for teachers to question existing structures and systems. Through an increased emphasis on stakeholder/school community involvement, the teachers at the case study school were enabled to make broader connections between different educational initiatives. For example, in the IQSA project they had to work in equal partnership with teachers from other schools and local and national advisors. In this process, the teachers began to experience a range of different viewpoints about what constituted an effective or inclusive school. These collaborative practices appeared to support the development of their reflective practice. They started to ask critical questions about so-called 'correct' or 'expected' models of policy and practice. In addition, they were working in partnership with advisors who were experiencing a similar process. Practice could now be explored more safely and teachers' professional identity was increasingly in question, as they began to ask, for example, 'What do I believe about this?' 'What is my role in school?' and, perhaps of fundamental importance, 'How do I think my students learn best?'

Through the IQSA project, the teachers at the case study school became involved in visits to other schools where they could share and observe other teachers who were trying out new ideas, which could then be adapted and 'tried out' back in school. As part of this project, schools visited each other locally and across the country. Learning during the visits was facilitated by national advisors and non-government organisations (NGO) project staff, who helped teachers to observe and discuss specific areas of pedagogy. Integral to this approach was a set of values which encouraged the teachers to be non-judgemental. Comparative education which focuses on good or bad practice is not necessarily the most useful in supporting teachers to change their own practice, rather teachers need to be encouraged to focus on 'pedagogy as ideas which enable teaching in the classroom, formalise it as policy and locate it in culture' (Alexander 2009: 10).

The role of the school principal is integral here. The research found that, where schools had principals who were focused on trying to develop their school and who saw supporting teachers as an integral part of this process, there was more likely to be sustainable change. Some of the school leaders were aware that teachers needed to understand new concepts, adapt them to their own context and take ownership of them in order for them to be sustainable. The principal of the case study school had clear views on this:

> We have learnt that you cannot watch somebody teach in another school and then take it back to your school to try and copy them. It doesn't seem to work that way … All children are different and so are teachers and schools. If you want to be a really inclusive school, then you need to understand that.
>
> (Case study school principal, Lao PDR)

The principal also had interesting insights into the way in which she felt she had needed to work in order to gain the trust of her colleagues when she became principal in 1995:

> I came to the school the year before I was made principal, as a deputy. The previous principal was a man and quite authoritarian. I didn't want to be like him because I knew that for our school to be a good one, I had to get the teachers to take ownership – so they couldn't see me as the one who made all the decisions. The first thing I did on the day I became principal was to go and clean the toilets. I think this was a message – I am one of you – we are all the same, we are equal.

In Trompenaars and Hampden-Turner's cultural typology (Trompenaars and Hampden-Turner 1997) and Hofstede's framework for assessing culture (Hofstede 2003) this can be interpreted as illustrating the second dimension: individualism and collectivism. In this case, the principal's actions can be located within the collectivist end of the dimension as she demonstrates publically her commitment to the group. She is also trying to build trust and create a sense of community where everyone is an individual but equal within the group. She goes on to say

> As principal I see it as my role to support the teachers in developing their skills – but I feel that the best way forward for this is to work together as a team. So, we plan together, sharing ideas, making resources and discussing issues in the school. Through the [IQSA project] we learnt about reflective practice – where we think about our teaching and ways in which we would like to change it. As an inclusive school this means that we are always trying to make sure that all our children are happy and fully participating in school. We believe that if this is the case then they will learn more effectively.
>
> (Case study school principal, Lao PDR, in Grimes 2009: 113)

This description of the role of the principal may not seem new or ground-breaking, but the significance can be understood only when seen in the context described above. The principal in the case study school was responding in a very specific, culturally informed way to her role. However, it would not be accurate to argue that this is typical of Lao PDR – it was only typical of this context, described in this case study. As I developed my research over a number of years, I began to assimilate that trying to understand cultural context in terms of so-called national identity was misleading and could lead to sweeping generalisations about factors which support the development of practice.

Similarly, 'local learning' for teachers could take place through unexpected developments at a local level, which did not necessarily fit in with preconceived expectations. The teachers in the case study school identified an intensive week-long trip to a primary school in Bangkok, Thailand as being particularly influential in developing their practice. As they came to know me and trust me as 'researcher', 'consultant' and 'critical friend', the teachers asked more about my research and whether they were the only school involved. The teachers in the Lao case study school very much wanted to visit the case study school in Thailand, described elsewhere (Grimes and Witoonchat 2005). Their motivation was multi-layered, including a wish to travel outside the country and to see the ocean for the first time, but I had no doubt that there was a real professional desire to learn from another context. Their trip to Bangkok was facilitated through external research funding, with an aim of encouraging and supporting critical 'learning conversations' where the teachers could spend time in classrooms observing new approaches to pedagogy and then discuss and share their impressions with the rest of the staff. All the teachers, the principal and two local education advisors made the trip and their learning conversations continued back in the school in Laos on their return home. In retrospect, the learning journey of the school can be seen as long and complex, but the visit to the case study school in Bangkok seemed to be a catalyst for changes in practice.

Some important points would seem to be that there was not a sense of copying what they observed elsewhere – it was discussed and made sense of in terms of their own context and local cultural environment. Key questions seemed to be 'How might this look in our classrooms?' and 'How does it ask us as teachers to think about ourselves differently?' Because of the collegiate approach to school development, described by the principal above, the teachers were able to explore these notions, together with the local advisors who were able to see the process from the inside and take my role as 'critical friend' on the school's learning journey.

Conclusion

My research findings would seem to support the importance of working within a framework which emphasises responding to local culture and context. The implication of this, as outlined above, is that those of us who work with and alongside teachers who are trying to develop their practice so that it responds to the needs and rights of all children, need to focus our energy on creating space for reflection and active exploration of practice. However, this 'space' must be located within and be responsive to the complexities of the values, expectations, social norms and experiences of the group and the community. The development of schools and the role of someone who positions themselves as a supporter, enabler, advisor or consultant is therefore enormously complex. It takes time and space to understand and is also very fragile. It is easy to create additional barriers to the development of inclusive practices through well-intentioned but badly thought through interventions or research methods. I have come to believe that the only realistic way to work with schools in communities is through a long-term ethnographic approach which enables and encourages listening, co-operation and trust. Understanding cultural factors and local context are the bedrock for this practice, but the researcher must never make the assumption that there is such a national culture or even identity. All culture is local and constructed by the individuals living and working within a setting or community.

Chapter 11

Leading on inclusion

The sum of the parts is not the whole story ...

John Cornwall

In this chapter I will attempt to sum up with attention to the particular perspectives that we set out to explore and have extracted through this writing and our work in this field over many years. Inclusion is an ephemeral construct that changes historically with social and cultural developments, and whilst we have attempted to outline debates, dilemmas and new perspectives, we should acknowledge that there will probably never be a 'whole story' or an endpoint to these debates. Nevertheless, we must analyse the past in order to create the future. Our hope is that this text will come across as a vehicle of creative ideas and of potential choices in action. Henri Bergson's philosophical take on this sums it up well:

> Time is what hinders everything from being given all at once. It is retardation. It must therefore be elaboration. Would it not then be a vehicle of creation and of choice? Would not the existence of time prove that there is indetermination in things? Would not time be that indetermination?
>
> (Bergson 1911: 110)

The pilot project that generated the initial ideas for this book was about strengthening the support that a child or young person with special needs and disabilities experiences in mainstream schools. It soon began to incorporate broader notions of inclusion and social change and we have further developed our ideas in this book. Up to 70 teachers took part in the pilot project and, in addition, my colleagues and I work with hundreds of practising teachers each year. The project also incorporated working with colleagues in special schools and availing ourselves of their knowledge and experience. Together, we wrestled with the many successes and issues of support and inclusion at school and classroom level. This daily and yearly experience, alongside our constant delving into research and evidence informed practice, has illuminated these perspectives. We also focus on the future of provision for pupils who do not conform to the pattern of normalisation and average expectations that has become synonymous with schooling. This book was not limited to the constraints that we experienced during the project and we raise further questions about the fundamental nature of the education system in the UK as a whole.

Early in the project (2006–7) it seemed that the notion of 'questioning' the status quo and the existence of certain apparently fixed characteristics of the UK education system was not an option. We were supposed to work within the boundaries set by the government, local and national. It was a challenge to introduce meaningful discourse around fundamental issues. It fitted with Kelly's (1990) earlier assertions that we actually have one of the most politically controlled education systems in the world. Yet we found, as a group of people committed to this task, that it was necessary to argue and confront traditional and non-evidence informed practices. It seems this is becoming more and more imperative as current political bandwagons begin to bite. Challenging received 'wisdom' is becoming a more and more essential part of developing better support for children in school who find it hard to engage with the narrow confines of learning that have been set up over the past 25 years or so. In the 1990s there was discussion about the state having a decreasing capacity for its role as an 'omniscient regulator' (Wagner 1994; Quicke 1997): it remains to be seen whether this role softens as proposed or whether it is really hardening its control in a covert fashion.

The book started with an historical and social perspective that has a distinctly circular tinge to it. It seems that, after nearly a century of activism, political wrangling and scientific development, we may be turning the clock back to a previous time: the time when being included in the education system was a privilege and not a civil and human right. Barnes (1990) sums up the way that our current inequality, often justified by fiscal arguments, has developed an inequality that is endemic in a school system that is becoming wholly part of the competitive and profit driven society:

> Whereas personal tragedy theory [of disability] over-emphasises subjective physiological and cognitive limitations through the professionally determined functional definitions of impairment, 'social reaction theory' challenged the authenticity of those definitions, but generally ignored the structural factors which may have necessitated or precipitated their application. While much attention is directed toward professional ineptitude and maladministration, little is paid to the structure itself. Such a position tends to ignore history and the stark inequalities of the free market economy.
>
> (Barnes 1990: 12)

Since 2003, efforts have been made, following the recommendation of the DfES investigation into the funding of SEN provision in schools and education elsewhere, to determine a fair funding situation. The *Report of the Special Schools Working Group* (DfES 2003d) proposed that the population of pupils with SEN was changing. Advances in medicine are allowing more children with complex health needs to survive well beyond school age; more children are being diagnosed with autistic spectrum disorders (ASD); and there is a growing number of children with severe behavioural, emotional and social difficulties. Set against this, the screening of newborn children for visual impairment and hearing impairment has allowed earlier intervention in these cases, which has reduced the impact of these disabilities. In 2011, the Green Paper produced by the Coalition Government espouses to 'respond to the frustrations of children and young people, their families and the professionals who work with them'. They have taken the view that continuing to provide and increase special-ist facilities is the way to ensure that children with additional needs and their families are catered for and missed the point that it is often the over-weaning bureaucracy and inflexibility of the education system that is the problem. The inflexibility created by dictatorial frameworks is based on the tired and ineffec-tive (over the past 20 years) efforts to 'drive up' standards. Ineffective because it has made little or no difference to standards but caused the system to become locked into a competitive accounting and non-learning centred mode.

There is no doubt that the movement towards more inclusive classrooms has made progress in the past 10–15 years, despite the movement towards a less equitable society. Following the British tradition of reactive politics, it has usu-ally been on the back of tragic events or disasters and an insurmountable wave of public opinion following them. Coming after *Every Child Matters*, there have been positive strides in local authorities that enable professionals work-ing in children's services to work more effectively in support of young people (Lord *et al.* 2008). There are ways forward and the authors in this book suggest and propose many of these. A movement to include the children's 'voice' in matters pertaining to their own schooling is described and suggestions devel-oped as to how this could be beneficial to all pupils including those with special educational needs. The point is raised that giving pupils a voice recognises their importance within the system and is part of all children's cultural and social development. Still, there are many unanswered questions about the equity of practice involving pupils with disabilities or disadvantages. Some of these ques-tions focus on in-school practices and some on the capability of outside bodies such as Ofsted to make judgements on such matters as pupil voice and special needs support for more complex disabilities. Other chapters in this book point to ways in which the classroom and whole school can be organised in a more inclusive fashion and others at specific elements within this. All of the chapters repeat a common theme summed up as the need for collaborative, explicit and evidence informed decision making in contrast to traditional, mythological and politically motivated decision making at all levels in the education system.

Tensions, change and competing ideologies

Many chapters in this book bring out quite clearly the now well-acknowledged tensions between educational paradigms that espouse competition, success and glittering academic prizes and those that are based on nurture, culture and human potential: Osler 2010; Ekins and Grimes 2009; Ainscow *et al.* 2006a; Cornwall and Walter 2006; Dyson *et al.* 2003 (inclusion agenda and standards debate); Cole 2005 (SENCOs as agents of change); Ball 2004. These tensions become apparent in competing agendas (MacBeath *et al.* 2006), leadership values and priorities pursued, in the way the classroom and school is organised, in the relationships between teachers (adults) and pupils (children and young people), in adhering to parochial as opposed to broad (perhaps international) perspectives and in priorities for training and continuing professional development. The international perspective indicates quite clearly the influence of a centrist, authoritarian government on teachers. These tensions and competing ideologies, whether 'industrial' educational paradigms that rest in the last century (Robinson 2011 [2001]) or resources limited by political agendas, constitute the context within which some pupils, senior managers and teachers are 'leading on inclusion'.

Commentators, authors and researchers (e.g. Cornwall 1995; Murphy 1996; Mason 2000; Fullan 2005; Cornwall and Walter 2006; Norwich 2010; Pearson 2010) have agreed for some time now that the attitudes generated by sets of beliefs and values are crucial to the way that a person behaves towards others. Teachers, support professionals and other educators are no exception to this notion. Researchers, authors and advocates also acknowledge that values can enter the research process at any point, influencing the focus of the research (i.e. what is important), the interpretation of the evidence and the use of research outcomes. In our current social and political set up, the national government and the European Union provide the largest amount of money to underpin social research and are clearly pursuing an agenda set by political imperatives (i.e. lobby groups and vote getting) and these are often contradictory and short term in their effect. Nevertheless, it is in the development of these personal and professional attitudes that one key must lie to making the changes that are sought by the whole concept of 'leading on inclusion'. Influencing national and local politics is one aspect, but working with colleagues within a smaller area of influence is also very important. This notion was borne out by comments made on the pilot study by teachers attempting to generate inclusive practices in their own and other schools and the outcomes of their researches:

> Children with complex needs and difficult behaviour are still difficult to include ... Still located in the medical model – i.e. it is often seen as all the child's fault and course participants have found it hard to tackle this with some colleagues in their school.

> Given the complex, contentious and contradictory nature of inclusion, it was initially difficult for participants to engage in critical discussion and debates around these issues. They usually held an over-simplistic and occasionally erroneous idea around inclusion, frequently reduced to a special education artefact. However, this 'conceptual misappropriation' around inclusion has been gradually reversed. Participants' thinking has changed and evolved towards a more critical understanding of the notion, informed

by the multiple and heterogeneous dynamics underpinning education policy and practice.

(Cornwall and Graham-Matheson 2008)

The 'industrial model' of current educational paradigms, so wonderfully portrayed by Sir Ken Robinson (2011 [2001]), is in stark contrast to the way that teachers are beginning to develop a collaborative whole staff approach built upon inclusive staff relationships. These working relationships within an inclusive culture of collaborative problem sharing rather than individual responsibility hold the key to both positive change and effective school development. Developing more flexible approaches towards teaching children through discussion supported by good evidence rather than accepted wisdoms is likely to produce teachers who can both experiment and evaluate with confidence.

> Working with a group that was already established and used to discussing issues and working collaboratively meant that we were able to move into the content very quickly ... encourages critical reflection rather than seeking to prescribe low level technical responses to need.
>
> (Cornwall and Graham-Matheson 2008)

The implication is that critical reflection, rather than tips for teachers (e.g. uninformed guidance such as in Cowley 2006) or low-level technical responses, will develop confident teachers who can solve problems. The popularity of such simplistic advice points to a gap in the way that young teachers are trained. The relative unpopularity of more serious discourse in the UK (in contrast to the way teachers in Europe and many other countries regard themselves) is a testament to the way that young teachers have been pushed into being 'followers' rather than initiators and professionals who can solve problems and lead others.

Leadership, bureaucracy and school development

Forward planning and strong leadership is seen as vital for developing effective and inclusive provision (DfES and DRC 2006). The various notions and issues surrounding what we call leadership have been discussed in previous chapters. What has come through very strongly is that leadership and leadership for inclusion is not all about the fixed hierarchical structures that exist within the education system. Like many areas of education (e.g. target setting), many notions of leadership have been imported from the business world. Unfortunately, some of the more old-fashioned ideas seem to have been pre-eminent over the past 20 years. These are traditional notions of authority, both in terms of executive power and control but also leaking into the classroom. The model of imposition of ideas, enforcers in schools and society and the need to 'police' teachers and their work has become endemic. This is not good or effective management by local and central government. It encourages disaffection and de-professionalises teachers. Knowledge has become an 'authority' all of its own and the academic class systems that exist militate against opportunity and learning for some. The notion of 'taking the lead' is a flexible socially based idea emanating perhaps from Émile Durkheim's (1897–8) original ideas of organic rather than mechanical solidarity in social systems. Those who hold executive powers and have responsibility for management seem to be terrified to allow freedom and organic development in the education system.

It has become clear in this book that to establish inclusive practices in schools raises something of a dilemma. Many commentators agree that it is not possible to develop an inclusive education system without radical school reform – or as other commentators say – not reform but complete transformation (Norwich 2010). In keeping with what has been discussed previously, it is not good enough for this reform to be a technocratic or even curriculum reform, but the inclusive discourse is about radical transformation of the school system. I have been personally committed to changing the education system for the past 25 years, before the inclusion debate became mainstream. However, the position prior to that was of 'equity', the human face of education, nurture and the encouragement of learning and culture in young people. It is not about exams, competition or even the race for jobs that, in all honesty, often do not match up to the aspirations of young people at school.

Placing all of the responsibility on to SENCOs for 'challenging complacency and relentlessly pursue the continual drive for further improvement' (Cheminais 2010) is a double-edged sword. In the early 1990s the problem of non-ownership existed. Teachers passed all of the responsibility for children with SEN or disabilities on to the backs of the SENCOs. In some schools this still exists but now the problem has changed. Placing SENCOs in an authoritarian hierarchy and characterising them as 'strategic leaders' risks producing another reaction that is akin to apathy or disaffection. There has been rejection of the notion of inclusion because it is seen partly as yet another initiative coming down from 'on high'. It is also seen as creating more work on the shoulders of teachers who are on the receiving end of too many top-down initiatives, some of which are highly confusing. On top of this, the overwhelming bureaucracy of reporting and accountability ('a tyranny of transparency', Ainscow 2005a) undermines SENCOs' ability to work more strategically (Pearson 2010). It reduces them to 'enforcers' or 'minders' when their true role should be as initiators and motivators, with the concomitant leadership and inter-personal skills necessary for inspiring colleagues.

Leading on inclusion – a summary

To summarise what has gone before:

- The changes that will bring about more inclusive practices in education (including those of higher education institutions that teach teachers) are transformational not transactional. Current hierarchies that exist between professionals and between staff in one institution will need to be replaced by heterarchies and a more collegiate ethos. This in turn means dispensing with the current ethos in education where things are 'driven' by enforcers for a new ethos of collaboration of socially and professionally equal partners. In short, a system that is more enabling and less competitively based on an old-fashioned industrial model.

- Competing ideologies, whether politically motivated or socially motivated, should give way to a more pragmatic approach. As long as the system 'drives' teachers and standards, teachers will be placed in the position of 'followers' and not the instigators they should be. Teachers have been thoroughly de-professionalised over the past 20 years by the unsuccessful 'drive' for narrow academic standards and the overwhelming bureaucracy that would make an accountant blush.

- Schools will become more inclusive and benefit more from a strategic approach that includes critical evaluation through setting up small collaborative research communities within schools. This means leaving behind the 'quick fix' ideologies and the low-level technical training 'en masse'. It means engaging with the evidence bases and the wider discourse that supports effective and person centred practices in education. It means leaving behind the notion of 'education for the masses' that developed in the Victorian era, and questioning the received wisdoms that come from various sources. Finally, it involves challenging the 'driven' culture that schools are currently subjected to.

To sum up, I would like to refer to enduring matters in the face of the rather ephemeral and misleading modern interpretations of what makes up education and society. To attempt to gain a perspective on what is going on at the moment, as we have done in this book. Education is about challenging and nurturing ALL young people and not just those to whom we attribute a narrow view of intelligence and capability. To develop an inclusive system is a journey not a destination and this is clear when we ask 'How far have we actually come since 1897?'

> I believe that the only true education comes through the stimulation of the child's powers by the demands of the social situations in which he finds himself. Through these demands he is stimulated to act as a member of a unity, to emerge from his original narrowness of action and feeling, and

to conceive of himself from the standpoint of the welfare of the group to which he belongs. Through the responses which others make to his own activities he comes to know what these mean in social terms. The value which they have is reflected back into them.

(Dewey 1897: article 1, page 1)

The move towards more inclusive practices in education is not just about minorities, it is about a better education for all and to achieve this it is becoming clear that the school and university system must be transformed – not just tinkered about with. The changes must be systemic and will only be effective when they are in concert with social and cultural changes. We are currently witnessing the power of people in the Arab world to change their political and social environment through sheer numbers of ordinary people expressing their views and sharing them. It is time for teachers to become more confident in their own professionality and not look to others to define what inclusion is, what good teaching is and what the role and characteristics of an effective teacher is.

Finally, Sir Ken Robinson, who chaired a government-commissioned inquiry in 1998, found that a prescriptive education system was stifling the creativity of teachers and their pupils. It is now 12 years later and he feels things have only got worse. Our approaches to education are 'stifling some of the most important capacities that young people now need to make their way in the increasingly demanding world of the twenty-first century – the powers of creative thinking' (quoted in Shepherd 2009).

It is my view that if we look to some of the things that will make education more satisfactory for everybody and respond to the natural and instinctive responses of young people (and older people who haven't forgotten what it's like to be young), then we are more likely to come up with an enduring notion of what education is for in the future. Inclusive education is more than just preparing the majority of young people at the most basic level – with the most basic of skills in a very narrow framework. This is accepting that the only role for education is to prepare for the most boring of jobs and a life that is dictated by the opinions and assessments of others. This was a criticism levelled at teachers of children with severe learning difficulties (low expectations) but is in fact endemic in the politicisation of the curriculum.

All children start their school careers with sparkling imaginations, fertile minds, and a willingness to take risks with what they think ... Most students never get to explore the full range of their abilities and interests ... Education is the system that's supposed to develop our natural abilities and enable us to make our way in the world. Instead, it is stifling the individual talents and abilities of too many students and killing their motivation to learn.

(Robinson, quoted in Shepherd 2009)

Sir Ken Robinson's very articulate arguments give clues as to how the current education system (at all levels) can make changes that will respond to his call for a more human-focused and creative school system. He suggests dispensing with the 'linear' system of rigid curricula and timetables, eliminating the hierarchy of subjects and encouraging a more flexible, creative approach to learning. In short, dispensing with the 'industrial' and Victorian model of education that we are still subject to in this modern age of social networking and complex communication systems. It is my view that this is what is necessary in order to make the transformation into a more inclusive education and school system. It will need to be a transformation that matches the technological advances with ethical, social and political changes.

References

Abbott, C. (2007) *E-inclusion: Learning Difficulties and Digital Technologies Bristol Futurelab.* Available at: http://archive.futurelab.org.uk/resources/documents/lit_reviews/Learning_Difficulties_Review2.pdf (accessed 12 May 2011).

Ainscow, M. (1994) *Creating the Conditions for School Improvement*, London: David Fulton.

—— (2002) *Understanding the Development of Inclusive Schools*, (Studies in Inclusive Education), London: RoutledgeFalmer.

—— (2005a) 'Developing inclusive education systems: what are the levers for change?' *Journal of Educational Change* 6(2) pp109–124.

—— (2005b) 'The next big challenge: inclusive school improvement', *International Congress of School Effectiveness and Improvement*, keynote presentation at the Conference of School Effectiveness and Improvement, Barcelona, January 2005.

—— (2007) 'Taking an inclusive turn', *Journal of Research in Special Educational Needs* 7(1) pp3–7.

Ainscow, M., Booth, T. and Dyson, A. (2006a) 'Inclusion and the standards agenda: negotiating policy pressures in England', *International Journal of Inclusive Education* 10(4–5) pp295–308.

Ainscow, M., Booth, T., Dyson, A., Howes, A., Gallannaugh, F., Smith, R., Farrell, P. and Frankham, J. (2006b) *Improving Schools, Developing Inclusion*, London: Routledge.

Ainslie, S., Foster, R., Groves, J., Grime, K., Straker, K. and Woolhouse, C. (2010) 'Making children count: an exploration of the implementation of the Every Child Matters agenda', *Education 3–13*, 38(1) pp23–38.

Aird, R. (2001) *The Education and Care of Children with Severe, Profound and Multiple Learning Difficulties*, London: David Fulton.

Alexander, R. (2009) 'Pedagogy, culture and the power of comparison', in H. Daniels, H. Lauder and J. Porter (eds) *Educational Theories, Cultures and Learning: A Critical Perspective*, Abingdon: Routledge.

Allan, J. (2003) *Inclusion, Participation and Democracy: What is the purpose?* Dordrecht, The Netherlands: Kluwer Academic Publishers.

—— (2005) 'Inclusion as an ethical project', in S. Tremain (ed.) *Foucault and the Government of Disability*, Michigan, IL: University of Michigan Press.

—— (2008) *Rethinking Inclusive Education: The Philosophers of Difference in Practice*, Dordrecht, The Netherlands: Springer.

Alliance for Inclusive Education (2005) 'Inclusion is Working' 2020 Campaign, Press release 9 March.

Altrichter, H., Feldman, A., Posch, P. and Somekh, B. (2007) *Teachers Investigate their Work: An Introduction to Action Research Across the Professions* (2nd edn), London: Routledge.

Anderson, V., Faraday, S., Prowse, S., Richards, G. and Swindells, D. (2003) *Count Me in FE*, London: Learning and Skills Development Agency.

Anning, A., Cottrell, D., Frost, N., Green, J. and Robinson, M. (2010) *Developing Multi-professional Teamwork for Integrated Children's Services* (2nd edn), Maidenhead: McGraw Hill/Open University Press.

Armstrong, D. (2005) 'Reinventing "inclusion": New Labour and the cultural politics of special education', *Oxford Review of Education* 31(1) pp135–151.

Armstrong, D., Armstrong, F. and Barton, L. (eds) (2000) *Inclusive Education: Policy, Contexts and Comparative Perspectives*, London: David Fulton.

Atkinson, M., Wilkin, A., Stott, A., Doherty, P. and Kinder, K. (2002) *Multi-Agency Working: A Detailed Study, LGA Research Report 26*, Slough: NFER.

Audit Commission (2002) *Statutory Assessment and Statements of SEN: In Need of a Review?* London: Audit Commission.

—— (2007) *Out of Authority Placements for Special Educational Needs*. London: Audit Commission.

Ball, S. (1993) 'What is Policy? Texts, Trajectories and Toolboxes', *Discourse* 13(2) pp10–17.

—— (2003) 'The teacher's soul and the terrors of performativity', *Journal of Educational Policy* 18(2) pp215–228.

—— (2004) 'Performativities and fabrications in the education economy: towards a perfomative society', in S. Ball (ed.) *The RoutledgeFalmer Reader in the Sociology of Education*, London: RoutledgeFalmer.

Balshaw, M. (2010) 'Looking for some different answers about teaching assistants', *European Journal of Special Needs Education* 25(4) pp337–338.

Barnes, C. (1990) *'Cabbage Syndrome': The Social Construction of Dependence*, London: Falmer Press.

Barnes, P. (2008) 'Multi-agency working: what are the perspectives of SENCOs and parents regarding its development and implementation?' *British Journal of Special Education* 35(4) pp230–240.

Barrett, A., Chawla-Duggan, R., Lowe, J. and Ukpo, E. (2006) *The Concept of Quality in Education: A Review of the International Literature on the Concept of Quality in Education*, Working Paper. EdQual RPC, (EdQual Working Paper: Quality No. 2).

Barton, L. (1988) (ed.) *The Politics of Special Education*, Lewes: Falmer Press.

—— (1993) 'The struggle for citizenship: the case of disabled people', *Disability, Handicap and Society* (8)3 pp235–246.

—— (1996) (ed.) *Disability and Society: Emerging Issues and Insights*, London: Addison Wesley Longman.

—— (1997) 'Inclusive education: romantic, subversive or realistic?' *International Journal of Inclusive Education* 1(3) pp231–242.

Barton, L. and Armstrong, F. (2007) (eds) *Policy, Experience and Change: Cross-cultural Reflections on Inclusive Education*, Dordrecht: Springer.

Becker, H. (1963) *Outsiders: Studies in the Sociology of Deviance*, New York: Free Press.

Bercow, J. (2008) *A Review of Services for Children and Young People (0–19) with Speech, Language and Communication Needs (The Bercow Report)*, Annesley: DCSF.

Bergson, H. (1911) *Creative Evolution*, New York: The Modern Library.

Biklen, D., Bogdan, R. and Blatt, B. (1977) 'Label jars not people', in M. Harmonay (ed.) *Promise and Performance: Children with Special Needs*, Action for Children's Television

Guide to Television Programming for Children, vol. 1, Cambridge, MA: Ballinger Publishing.

Black, P. and William, D. (2006) 'Developing a theory of formative assessment', in J. Garner (ed.) *Assessment and Learning*, London: Sage.

Black-Hawkins, K., Florian, L. and Rowe, M. (2007) *Achievement and Inclusion in Schools*, Abingdon: Routledge.

Booth, T. (1983) 'Integrating Special Education', in T. Booth and P. Potts (eds) *Integrating Special Education*, Oxford: Blackwell.

—— (1999) 'Viewing inclusion from a distance: gaining perspective from comparative studies', *Support for Learning* 14(4) pp164–168.

Booth, T. and Ainscow, M. (2002) *Index for Inclusion: Developing Learning and Participation in Schools*, Bristol: Centre for Studies on Inclusive Education.

Boxall, M. (2002) *Nurture Groups in Schools: Principles and Practice*, London, Sage/Paul Chapman.

Brackenreed, D. (2008) 'Inclusive education: identifying teachers' perceived stressors in inclusive classrooms', *Exceptionality Education*, Canada, 18(3) pp131–147.

British Dyslexia Association (2010) *Dyslexia Friendly Schools*. Available at: http://www.bdadyslexia.org.uk/quality-mark-and-accreditation.html (accessed 8 June 2011).

British Educational Research Association (2004) *Revised Ethical Guidelines for Educational Research*, Nottingham: BERA.

British Psychological Society (2005) *Submission to House of Commons Select Committee Inquiry* (5.4: 4).

Bronfenbrenner, U. (1970) *Two Worlds of Childhood: US and USSR*, New York: Sage.

Bunting, I. A. (1993) 'Rationalisation, quality and efficiency', *South African Journal of Higher Education* 7(2) pp17–27.

Buse, K. (2005) *Education for All – Fast Track Initiative: Review of the Governance and Management Structures*, London: Overseas Development Institute.

Cedillo, I. and Fletcher, T. (2010) 'Attending to diversity: a professional learning program in Mexico', in C. Forlin (ed.) *Teacher Education for Inclusion: Changing Paradigms and Innovative Approaches*, Abingdon: Routledge.

Centre for Studies on Inclusive Education (2005) *Are LEAs in England Abandoning Inclusive Education?* Press release 8 July, CSIE. Available at: http://inclusion.uwe.ac.uk/csie/segregationstats2005.htm (accessed 6 June 2011).

Charlton, J. (1998) *Nothing About Us Without Us*, London: University of California Press.

Chawla-Duggan, R. (2007) 'Breaking out, breaking through: accessing knowledge in a non-western overseas educational setting – methodological issues for an outsider', *Compare* 37(2) pp185–200.

Cheminais, R. (2005) *Every Child Matters: a New Role for SENCOs*, London: David Fulton.

—— (2010) *Rita Cheminais' Handbook for New SENCOs*, London: Sage.

Clark, C., Dyson, A. and Millward, A. (1998) 'Theorising special education: time to move on?' in C. Clark, A. Dyson and A Millward *Theorising Special Education*, London: Routledge.

Clough, P. and Corbett, J. (2006) *Theories of Inclusive Education: A Students' Guide*, London: Paul Chapman.

Cole, B. (2005) 'Mission impossible? Special educational needs, inclusion and the re-conceptualisation of the role of the SENCO in England and Wales', *European Journal of Special Needs Education* 20(3) pp287–307.

Corbett, J. (2001) *Supporting Inclusive Education*, London: RoutledgeFalmer.

Cornwall, J. (1995) *Choice, Opportunity and Learning: Educating Children and Young People Who are Physically Disabled*, London: David Fulton.

Cornwall, J. and Graham-Matheson, L. (2008) *TDA Pilot Project: Strengthening the Specialist SEN Expertise of Serving Teachers*, Final report, October, Report of the work of the Consortium of Higher Education Institutions (unpublished).

Cornwall, J. and Walter, C. (2006) *Therapeutic Education: Working Alongside Children Who Are Troubled and Troublesome*, London: David Fulton.

Cowley, S. (2006) *Getting the Buggers to Behave*, London: Continuum.

Cowne, E. (2003) *The SENCO Handbook: Working Within a Whole School Approach* (4th edn), London: David Fulton.

Croll, P. and Moses, D. (2000) 'Ideologies and utopias: education professionals' view of inclusion', *European Journal of Special Needs Education* 15(1) pp1–12.

Crossley, M. and Vulliamy, G. (1998) (eds) *Qualitative Educational Research in Developing Countries: Current Perspectives, Reference Books in International Education* series, London: Routledge.

Cullingford, C. (2005) 'Lessons from learners about inclusive curriculum and pedagogy', in M. Nind, J. Rix, K. Sheeey and K. Simmons (eds) *Curriculum and Pedagogy in Inclusive Education*, London: Routledge.

Darby, A. and Fairley, A. (2002) *Inclusion: What Young People Tell Us*, Nottingham: Nottingham City Council.

Davis, M. (1992) Professional Judgment: Perspectives on the Professions 11(2). Available at: http://www.sciencedirect.com/science/article/pii/S0742051X0800111X (accessed 29 April 2009).

Day, C. (2004) *A Passion for Teaching*, London: RoutledgeFalmer.

Day, C., Kington, A., Stobart, G. and Sammons, P. (2006) 'The personal and professional selves of teachers: stable and unstable identities', *British Educational Research Journal* 32(4) p601–616.

Day, J. (1995) *Access Technology: Making the Right Choice* (2nd edn), NCET: Coventry.

Dempster, N. (2009) 'What do we know about leadership?' in J. MacBeath and N. Dempster (eds) *Connecting Leadership and Learning: Principles for Practice*, London: Routledge.

Department for Children, Schools and Families (2007a) *Guidance on the Duty to Promote Community Cohesion*, London: DCSF.

—— (2007b) *Social and Emotional Aspects of Learning*, London: DCSF.

—— (2007c) *Primary National Strategy: Pupil Progress Meeting Prompts and Guidance*, London: DCSF.

—— (2008a) *The National Strategies*, London: DCSF.

—— (2008b) *The 21st Century School: A Transformation in Education*, London: DCSF.

—— (2009) *Designing for Disabled Children and Children with Special Educational Needs: Guidance for Mainstream and Special Schools, Building Bulletin 102*, November 2009, Norwich: The Stationery Office.

Department for Children, Schools and Families/Department of Health (2008) *Children and Young People in Mind: The Final Report of the National CAMHS Review*, London: DCSF.

Department for Education (1994) *Code of Practice on the Identification and Assessment of Pupils with Special Educational Needs*, London: DfE.

—— (2010) *The Importance of Teaching – The Schools White Paper 2010*, London: DfE.

—— (2011a) *Special Educational Needs in England January 2010*. Available at: http://www.education.gov.uk/rsgateway/DB/SFR/s000939/index.shtml (accessed 15 May 2011).

—— (2011b) *Support and Aspiration: A New Approach to Special Educational Needs and Disability*, Green Paper, Norwich: TSO.

Department for Education and Employment (1995) *Disability Discrimination Act 1995*, London: HMSO.

—— (1997) *Excellence for All Children: Meeting Special Educational Needs*, London: DfEE.

Department for Education and Employment/Qualifications and Curriculum Authority (1999) *Inclusion: Providing Effective Learning Opportunities for all Children, in the National Curriculum Handbook for Primary/Secondary Teachers in England*, London: DfEE/QCA.

Department for Education and Skills (2000) *Working With Teaching Assistants: A Good Practice Guide*, London: DfES.

—— (2001a) *Special Educational Needs Code of Practice*, Annesley: DfES.

—— (2001b) *Inclusive Schooling: Children with Special Educational Needs*, London: DfES.

—— (2003a) *Every Child Matters*, Green Paper, London: DfES.

—— (2003b) *Excellence and Enjoyment: A Strategy for Primary Schools*, London: DfES.

—— (2003c) *Towards a Unified e-Learning Strategy: Consultation Document*, Annesley: DfES.

—— (2003d) *Report of the Special Schools Working Group (Executive Summary)*, Nottingham: DfES.

—— (2004a) *Removing Barriers to Achievement – The Government's Strategy for SEN*. Annesley: DfES.

—— (2004b) *Every Child Matters: Change for Children*, London: DfES.

—— (2004c) *Working Together: Giving Young People a Say*, Annesley: DfES.

—— (2004d) *Every Child Matters: Next Steps*, London: DfES.

—— (2004e) *Five Year Strategy for Children and Learners*, London: DfES.

—— (2005a) *Common Assessment Framework for Children and Young People: Guide for Service Managers and Practitioners*, London: DfES.

—— (2005b) *Lead Professional Good Practice Guidance for Children with Additional Needs*, London: DfES.

—— (2005c) *Draft Standards for SEN Support and Outreach Services*, London: DfES.

—— (2005d) *Every Child Matters: Outcomes Framework*, London: DfES.

—— (2005e) *Higher Standards, Better Schools for All*, Annesley: DfES

—— (2006) 'Creating an inclusive classroom-learning environment', in Primary National Strategy. Available at: http://nationalstrategies.standards.dcsf.gov.uk/node/ 46806?uc =force_uj (accessed 8 June 2011).

—— (2007a) *Social and Emotional Aspects of Learning (SEAL)*, Nottingham: DfES.

—— (2007b) *2020 Vision: Report of the Teaching and Learning in 2020 Review Group*, London: DfES.

Department for Education and Skills/Disability Rights Commission (2006) *Implementing the Disability Discrimination Act in Schools and Early Years Settings*, Nottingham: DfES.

Department of Education and Science (1978) *Special Educational Needs: Report of the Committee of Enquiry into the Education of Handicapped Children and Young People (The Warnock Report)*, Cmnd 7212, London: HMSO.

Department of Education, Northern Ireland. (2005) *School Development Planning: Investors in People*. Available at: http://www.belb.org.uk/Downloads/gov_guidance.pdf (accessed 8 June 2011).

Department of Health (1989) *The Children Act*, London: HMSO.

Department of Health and Social Services (1976) *Fit for the Future: The Report of the Committee on Child Health Service* (The Court Report), Cmnd 6684, London: DHSS.

Deppeler, J. (2010) 'Professional learning as collaborative enquiry: working together for impact', in C. Forlin (ed.) *Teacher Education for Inclusion: Changing Paradigms and Innovative Approaches*, London: Routledge.

DiPaola, M. and Walther-Thomas, C. (2003) *Principals and Special Education: The Critical Role of School Leaders* (COPPSE Document No. IB-7), Gainesville, FL: University of Florida, Centre on Personnel Studies in Special Education.

Dewey, J. (1897) 'My pedagogic creed', *The School Journal*, LIV(3), 16 January, pp77–80.

—— (1933) *How we Think: A Restatement of the Relation of Reflective Thinking to the Educative Process*, Boston: Heath.

—— (1944) *Democracy and Education: An Introduction to the Philosophy of Education*, New York: The Free Press.

Dottin, E. S. (2009) 'Professional judgment and dispositions in teacher education', *Teaching and Teacher Education* 25 pp83–88.

Durham, M. (1992) 'When is learning difficulty a handicap? When it confuses the public', The *Independent*, 18 October.

Durkheim, É. (1897–8) 'De la définition des phénomènes religieux', *L'Année Sociologique* 2 pp1–28.

Dyson, A. (2001) 'Special needs in the twenty-first century: where we've been and where we're going', *British Journal of Special Education* 28(1) pp24–29.

—— (2005) 'Philosophy, politics and economics? The story of inclusive education in England', in D. Mitchell *Contextualising Inclusive Education: Evaluating Old and New International Perspectives*, London: Routledge.

Dyson, A. and Millward, A. (1997) 'The reform of special education or the transformation of mainstream schools', in S. Pijl, C. Meijer and S. Hegarty (eds) *Inclusive Education: A Global Agenda*, London: Routledge.

Dyson, A., Gallannaugh, F. and Millward, A. (2003) 'Making space in the standards agenda: developing inclusive practices in schools,' *European Educational Research Journal* 2 pp228–244.

Dyson, A., Howes, A. and Roberts, B. (2002) 'A systematic review of the effectiveness of school-level actions for promoting participation by all students', in Research Evidence in Education Library, London: EPPI-Centre, Social Science Research Unit, Institute of Education, University of London. Available at: http://eppi.ioe.ac.uk (accessed 8 June 2011).

Edmunds, A. and Macmillan, R. (eds) (2010) *Leadership for Inclusion*, Rotterdam: Sense Publishers.

Egerton Commission (1889) *Report of the Royal Commission on the Blind, the Deaf, the Dumb and Others of the United Kingdom*, 4 vols, London: HMSO (in Riddell 2002).

Ekins, A. (2010) 'An exploration of developing inclusive practices in schools: case studies of two primary schools', unpublished doctoral thesis, University of Kent/Canterbury Christ Church University.

Ekins, A. and Grimes, P. (2009) *Inclusion: Developing an Effective Whole School Approach*, Maidenhead: Open University Press.

Ellis, S., Tod, J. and Graham-Matheson, L. (2008) *Special Education Needs and Inclusion: Reflection and Renewal*, Birmingham: NASUWT.

Ely, M., Anzul, M., Friedman, T., Garner, D. and McCormack-Steinmetz, A. (1991) *Doing Qualitative Research: Circles within Circles*, London: Falmer Press.

Evans, J. and Lunt, I. (2002) 'Inclusive education: are there limits?' *European Journal of Special Needs Education* 17(1) pp1–14.

Farrell, P. and Ainscow, M. (eds) (2002) *Making Special Education Inclusive*, London: David Fulton.

Florian, L. and Linklater, H. (2010) 'Preparing teachers for inclusive education: using inclusive pedagogy to enhance teaching and learning for all', *Cambridge Journal of Education* 40(4) pp369–386.

Forbes, F. (2007) 'Towards inclusion: an Australian perspective', *Support for Learning* 22(2) pp66–67.

Foundation for People with Learning Disabilities (2008) *What About Us? Promoting Emotional Well-being and Inclusion by Working with Young People with Learning Difficulties in Schools and Colleges*, London: Mental Health Foundation.

Frederickson, N. and Cline, T. (2009) *Special Educational Needs, Inclusion and Diversity*, Maidenhead: Open University Press.

Freeman, M. (2010) 'Why it remains important to take children's rights seriously', in J. Rix, M. Nind, K. Sheehy, K. Simmons and C. Walsh *Equality, Participation and Inclusion 1: Diverse Perspectives*, Abingdon: Routledge.

Frith, U. and Happé, F. (1994) 'Autism: beyond "theory of mind"', *Cognition* 50 pp115–132.

Frost, N. (2005) *Professionalism, Partnership and Joined Up Thinking*, Dartington: Research in Practice.

Fuchs, D. and Fuchs, L. (1994) 'Inclusive school movement and the radicalisation of special education reform', *Exceptional Children*, 60(4) pp294–309.

Fulcher, G. (1999) *Disabling Policies? A Comparative Approach to Education Policy and Disability*, London: Falmer Press.

Fullan, M. (2004) *Leading in a Culture of Change: Personal Action Guide and Workbook*, San Francisco, CA: Jossey-Bass.

—— (2005) *Leadership and Sustainability*, Bedfordshire: NCSL.

—— (2006) 'The future of educational change: system thinkers in action', *Journal of Educational Change* 7 pp113–122.

Gillborn, D. and Youdell, D. (2000) *Rationing Education*, Maidenhead: Open University Press.

Glenny, G. and Roaf, C. (2008) *Multi-professional Communication: Making Systems Work for Children*, Maidenhead: McGraw Hill/Open University Press.

Grimes, P. (2009) *A Quality Education for All: the History of the Lao PDR Inclusive Education Project 1993–2009*, Vientiane: Save the Children.

Grimes, P. and Witoonchat, M. (2005) 'Developing innovative inclusive practice at Meanprasatwittaya school in Bangkok, Thailand', *2nd International Conference on Inclusive Education, December 2005*, Hong Kong: Hong Kong Institute of Education.

Grimes, P., Sayarath, K. and Outhaithany, S. (2007) 'The development of the Lao PDR school self evaluation tool', *International Congress for School Effectiveness and Improvement*, Portoroz, Slovakia: ICSEI.

—— (2009a) 'Improving the quality of schools for all: researching the impact of the Lao PDR inclusive education project 1993–2008', *International Congress for School Effectiveness and Improvement*, Vancouver, Canada: ICSEI.

—— (2009b) 'The Lao PDR inclusive education project 1993–2009: reflections on policy evolving into practice', 10th UKFIET International Conference on Education and Development, Oxford.

Grimes, P., Stevens, M., Nguyen, T. and Sayarath, K. (2010) 'Inclusive education in South East Asia: critical challenges in Vietnam, Lao PDR and Cambodia', Australian Disability and Development Consortium Conference 'Implementing Disability-inclusive Development in the Pacific and Asia', Australia: Darwin Convention Centre.

Gwynn, J. (2004) 'What about Me? I live here too!' in F. Armstrong and M. Moore (eds) *Action Research for Inclusive Education, Changing Places, Changing Practices, Changing Minds*, London: RoutledgeFalmer.

Hall, J. (1997) *Social Devaluation and Special Education: The Right to Full Mainstream Inclusion and an Honest Statement*, London: Jessica Kingsley.

Hallam, S., Castle, F. and Rogers, L. (2004) *Research and Evaluation of Behaviour Improvement Programmes*, interim report, London: Institute of Education.

Hallett, F. and Hallet, G. (eds) (2010) *Transforming the role of the SENCO: Achieving the National Award for SEN Co-ordination*, Maidenhead: Open University Press.

Hallett, F., Hallett, G. and McAteer, M. (2007) 'Every voice matters: evaluating residential provision at a special school', *British Journal of Special Education*, 34 pp219–225.

Hammarbeg, T. (1997) 'A school for children with rights: the significance of the United Nations Convention on the Rights of the Child for modern education policy', *Innocenti Lecture*, Sala Giunta della Presidenza Regionale Palazzo Bastogi, Florence, Italy: UNICEF.

Hanko, G. (1999) *Increasing Competence through Collaborative Problem Solving*, London: David Fulton.

Hansen, D. (2000) 'Teaching as a moral activity', in V. Richardson (ed.) *Handbook of Research on Teaching* (4th edn), Washington, DC: American Educational Research Association.

—— (2001) *Exploring the Moral Heart of Teaching*, New York: Teachers College Press.

Hardy, C. (2000) *Information Communication Technology for All*, London: David Fulton.

Harris, A. (2008) *Distributed Leadership in Schools: Developing the Leaders of Tomorrow*, London: RoutledgeFalmer.

Harris, A. and Spillane, J. (2008) 'Distributed leadership through the looking glass', *Management in Education* 22 pp31–34.

Hartley, L. P. (1953) *The Go-Between*, London: Hamish Hamilton.

Heifetz, R. (1994) *Leadership Without Easy Answers*, Cambridge, MA: Harvard University Press.

HMSO (2001) *Special Educational Needs and Disability Act*, London: HMSO.

Hodkinson, A. (2010) 'Inclusive and special education in the English educational system: historical perspectives, recent developments and future challenges', *British Journal of Special Education* 37(32) pp61–67.

Hofstede, G. (2003) *Cultures and Organisations: Software of the Mind*, London: Profile Books.

Holdsworth, J. (2003) *Seeking a Fine Balance: Lessons from Inclusive Education in Lao PDR*, Vientiane: Save the Children.

Holt, M. (2000) 'Introduction: the concept of quality in education', in C. Hoy, C. Bayne-Jardin and M. Wood (eds) *Improving Quality in Education*, London: Falmer.

Hope, M. (1986) *The Magic of the Micro: a Resource for Children with Learning Difficulties*, London: CET.

—— (1987) *Micros for Children with Special Needs*, London: Souvenir Press.

Hornby, G., Davis, G. and Taylor, G. (1995) *Special Educational Needs Co-ordinator's Handbook*, London: Routledge.

House of Commons Education and Skills Select Committee (2006) *Report on Special Educational Needs*, London: TSO.

House of Commons Merits of Statutory Instruments Committee (2009) Education (Special Educational Needs Co-ordinators) (England) (Amendment) Regulations 2009. Available at: http://www.publications.parliament.uk/pa/ld200809/ldselect/ldmerit/122/12203.htm (accessed 9 September 2011).

Howes, A., Davies, S. and Fox, S. (2009a) *Improving the Context for Inclusion Through Collaborative Action Research*, London: Routledge.

Howes, A., Grimes, P. and Shohel, M.M.C. (2009b) 'Imagining inclusive teachers: contesting policy assumptions in relation to the development of inclusive practice in schools', 10th UKFIET International Conference on Education and Development, Oxford.

Huberman, A. M. and Miles, M. B. (1984) *Innovation Up Close: How School Improvement Works*, New York: Plenum Press.

Huxham, C. and Vangen, S. (2005) *Managing to Collaborate: The Theory and Practice of Collaborative Advantage*, London: Routledge.

Jones, P. (2005) 'Inclusion: lessons from the children', *British Journal of Special Education* 32(2) pp60–67.

Judge, S., Floyd, K. and Jeffs, T. (2008) 'Using an assistive technology toolkit to promote inclusion', *Early Childhood Education Journal*, 36(2) pp121–126.

Keates, C. (2010) Address to NASUWT Annual Conference. BBC News 3 April 2010. Available at: http://news.bbc.co.uk/1/hi/education/8602133.stm (accessed 8 June 2011).

Kelly, A. (1990) *The National Curriculum: A Critical Review* (1994 Update), London: Paul Chapman.

Kenworthy, J. and Whittaker, J. (2000) 'Anything to declare? The struggle for inclusive education and children's rights', *Disability and Society* 15(2) pp219–231.

King, K. (2007) 'Multilateral agencies in the construction of the global agenda on education', *Comparative Education* 43(3) pp377–391.

Koster, M., Pijl, S., Nakken, H., and Van Houten, E. (2010) 'Social participation of students with special needs in regular primary education in the Netherlands', *International Journal of Disability, Development and Education* 57 pp59–75.

Kozik, P., Cooney, P., Vinciguerra, S. and Gradel, K. (2009) 'Promoting inclusion in secondary schools through appreciative inquiry', *American Secondary Education* 38(1) Fall 2009.

Kugelmas, J. (2003) *Inclusive Leadership: Leadership for Inclusion*, Nottingham: NCSL.

Kumar, K. (2010) 'A journey towards creating an inclusive classroom: how universal design for learning has transformed my teaching', *Transformative Dialogues: Teaching and Learning Journal* 4(2). Available at: http://kwantlen.ca/TD/TD.4.2/TD.4.2.5_Kumar_Inclusive_Classroom.pdf (accessed 9 September 2011).

Lacey, P. (2001) *Support Partnerships: Collaboration in Action*, London: David Fulton.

Lamb, B. (2009) *The Lamb Inquiry: Special Educational Needs and Parental Confidence*, Annesley: DCSF.

Lauchlan, F. and Boyle, C. (2007) 'Is the use of labels in special education helpful?' *Support for Learning* 22 pp36–42.

Lave, J. and Wenger, E. (1991) *Situated Learning: Legitimate Peripheral Participation*, Cambridge: Cambridge University Press.

Layton, L. (2005) 'Special educational needs co-ordinators and leadership: a role too far?' *Support for Learning* 20(2) pp34–52.

Lee, H. and Templeton, R. (2008) 'Ensuring equal access to technology: providing assistive technology for students with disabilities', *Theory Into Practice* 47(3) pp212–219.

Lethard, A. (ed.) (1994) *Going Inter-professional: Working Together for Health and Welfare*, London: Routledge.

Liabo, K., Newman, T., Stephens, J. and Lowe, K. (2001) *A Review of Key Worker Systems for Disabled Children and the Development of Information Guides for Parents, Children and Professionals*, Cardiff: Wales Office for R&D Health & Social Care.

Lingard, B. and Mills, M. (2007) 'Pedagogies making a difference: issues of social justice and inclusion', *International Journal of Inclusive Education* 11(3) pp233–244.

Liston, A., Nevin, A., and Malian, I. (2009) 'What do paraeducators in inclusive classrooms say about their work? Analysis of national survey data and follow-up interviews in California', *TEACHING Exceptional Children Plus* 5(5) pp2–17.

Lloyd, C. (2008) 'Removing barriers to achievement: a strategy for inclusion or exclusion?', *International Journal of Inclusive Education* 12(2) pp221–236.

Lord, P., Kinder, K., Wilkin, A., Atkinson, M. and Harland, J. (2008) *Evaluating the Early Impact of Integrated Children's Services: Round 1 Final Report*, Slough: NFER.

Loreman, T. (2010) 'Exploring beliefs about teaching students with cognitive disabilities', in B. Uditsky and A. Hughson (eds) *Teaching Students with Mild/Moderate or Severe Cognitive Disabilities in Inclusive Schools*, Grades 1–12, Alberta: Alberta Education.

Loreman, T. J., Deppeler, J. M. and Harvey, D. (2010) *Inclusive Education: Supporting Diversity in the Classroom* (2nd edn) London: Routledge.

Lorenz, S. (2002) *First Steps in Inclusion*, London: David Fulton.

Low, C. (1996) 'Sense and nonsense relocated in special educational needs', Policy Options Group (ed.) *Provision for Special Educational Needs from the Perspectives of Service Users*, Tamworth: NASEN.

Loxley, A. and Thomas, G. (2001) 'Neo-conservatives, neo-liberals, the New Left and inclusion: stirring the pot', *Cambridge Journal of Education* 341(3) pp291–301.

Lundy, L. (2007) 'Voice is not enough: conceptualising Article 132 of the United Nations Convention on the Rights of the Child', *British Educational Research Journal* 33(6) pp927–942.

Lynas, W. (2002) 'Specialist teachers and inclusion: a case study of teachers of the deaf working in mainstream schools', in P. Farrell and M. Ainscow (eds) *Making Special Education Inclusive*, London: David Fulton.

MacBeath, J. (2006) *School Inspection and Self-evaluation: Working with the New Relationship*, London: RoutledgeFalmer.

MacBeath, J., Galton, M., Steward, S., MacBeath, A. and Page, C. (2006) *Costs of Inclusion: A study of Inclusion Policy and Practice in English Primary, Secondary and Special Schools*, Cambridge: University of Cambridge/National Union of Teachers.

MacGilchrist, B., Reed, J. and Myers, K. (2004) *The Intelligent School* (2nd edn), London: Sage.

MacIntyre, D. (2010) 'Has classroom teaching served its day?' in J. Rix, M. Nind, K. Sheehy, K. Simmons and C. Walsh *Equality, Participation and Inclusion 1. Diverse Perspectives*, Abingdon: Routledge.

MacKeith, M. (2010) 'HobNob: getting together to talk or not, one for all'. Available at: www.one-for-all.org.uk (accessed 8 March 2011).

MacKenzie, S. (2007) 'A review of recent developments in the role of the SENCO in the UK', *British Journal of Special Education* 34(4) pp212–218.

MacLean, M. (2008) 'Teaching about disability: an ethical responsibility?' *International Journal of Inclusive Education* 12(5) pp605–619.

Mason, M. (2000) Interview with G. Richards, 'disability, equal opportunities and initial teacher training in further education: will current approaches promote inclusion?' unpublished doctoral thesis, University of Sheffield.

—— (2005) *Incurably Human*, Nottingham: Inclusive Solutions.

—— (2011) 'Thinking about the oppression of people with learning difficulties', *Inclusion Now*, 28 pp14–15.

McLaughlin, C. (2008) 'Emotional well-being and its relationship to schools and classrooms: a critical reflection', *British Journal of Guidance and Counselling* 36(4) pp353–366.

McLaughlin, M. (2009) *What Every Principal Needs to Know About Special Education*, Thousand Oaks, CA: Corwin Press.

Mencap (2011) Mencap Homepage. Available at: www.mencap.org.uk (accessed 7 March 2011).

Middlemas, B. (2009) 'Using a student voice approach to develop more inclusive and diverse ways of assessing coursework', Napier University, Hearing the Student Voice Project. Available at: http://www.seda.ac.uk/resources/files/20_Middlemas.pdf (accessed 9 September 2011).

—— (2010) *Interviews with 25 New to Post SENCOs*, unpublished study, Roehampton University.

—— (2011) *Learning and Teaching in the Biosciences*, unpublished doctoral thesis, Roehampton University.

Milbourne, L. (2005) 'Children, families and inter-agency work: Experiences of partnership work in primary education settings', *British Educational Research Journal* 31(6) pp675-695.

Miles, S. and Singal, N. (2010) 'The education for all and inclusive education debate: conflict, contradiction or opportunity?' *International Journal of Inclusive Education* 14(1) pp1–15.

Ministry of Education (2008) *Lao PDR Education For All Mid Decade Assessment*, Ventiane: Lao PDR.

—— (2009) *Education Sector Development Framework in Lao PDR*, Ventiane: Lao PDR.

Mitchell, D. (2008) *What Really Works in Special and Inclusive Education: Using Evidence-Based Teaching Strategies*, London: Routledge.

Mittler, P. (2000) *Working Towards Inclusive Education: Social Contexts*, London: David Fulton.

Moran, D. and Abbott, L. (2002) 'Developing inclusive schools: the pivotal role of teaching assistants in promoting inclusion in special and mainstream schools in Northern Ireland', *European Journal of Special Needs Education* 17(2) pp161–173.

Morgan, H. and Byers, R. (2008) *Inclusion Policy*, London: Council for Disabled Children/ National Children's Bureau.

Morris, J. (1992) in Barton, L. (2010) 'The politics of education for all', in J. Rix, M. Nind, K. Sheehy, K. Simmons and C. Walsh *Equality, Participation and Inclusion 1. Diverse Perspectives*, Abingdon: Routledge.

Morrow, V. (2006) 'We get played for fools. Some promises and pitfalls of community and institutional participation for children and young people', keynote speech, Pupil Voice and Participation: Pleasures, promises and Pitfalls, National Research Conference, Nottingham University.

Mortimore, P. and Whitty, G. (2000) *Can School Improvement Overcome the Effects of Disadvantage?* London: Institute of Education, University of London.

Moss, G., Jewitt, C., Levacic, R., Armstrong, V., Cardini, A. and Castle, F. (2007) *The Interactive Whiteboards, Pedagogy and Pupil Performance Evaluation*, London: DfES.

Mott, G. (2004) *Children at the Heart: Vision into Action*, EMIE Report 84, Slough: NFER.

Murphy, D. (1996) 'Implications of inclusion for general and special education', *Elementary school Journal* 96 pp469–93.

National College for School Leadership (2004) *Distributed Leadership*, Nottingham: NCSL.

—— (2005) *Towards the e-Confident School*. Available at: 3c9s.e2bn.net/.../essential_guides_econfident_school%5B1%5D.pdf (accessed 12 May 2011).

Nguyen, P., Elliott, J., Terlouw, C. and Pilot, A. (2009) 'Neo-colonialism in education: co-operative learning in an Asian context', *Comparative Education* 45(1) pp109–130.

Nias, J., Southwark, G. and Yeomans, R. (1989) *Staff Relationships in the Primary School*, London: Cassell Educational.

Nind, M. (2005) 'Introduction: models and practice in inclusive curricula', in M. Nind, J. Rix, K. Sheehy and K. Simmons (eds) *Curriculum and Pedagogy in Inclusive Education: Values into Practice*, Abingdon: RoutledgeFalmer/Open University Press.

Norwich, B. (1996) 'Special needs education or education for all: connective specialisation and ideological impurity', *British Journal of Special Education* 23(3) pp100–104.

—— (2010) 'A response to special educational needs: a new look', in L. Terzi (ed.) *Special Educational Needs: A New Look*, London: Continuum.

Ntombela, S. (2011) 'The progress of inclusive education in South Africa: teachers' experiences in a selected district, KwaZulu-Natal', *Improving Schools* 14(1) pp5–14.

Office for Standards in Education (2000) *Evaluating Educational Inclusion*, London: Ofsted.

—— (2002) *ICT in Schools: The Impact of Government Initiatives*, London: Ofsted.

—— (2003) *Special Educational Needs in the Mainstream*, London: Ofsted.

—— (2004) *Special Educational Needs and Disability: Towards Inclusive Schools*, London: HMSO.

—— (2006) *Inclusion: Does it Matter Where Pupils are Taught?* London: HMSO.

—— (2010a) *The Special Educational Needs and Disability Review: A Statement is Not Enough*, London: Ofsted.

—— (2010b) *The Special Educational Needs and Disability Review, Report Summary*, Manchester: Ofsted.

—— (2011) *Special Educational Needs and/or Disabilities in Mainstream Schools: A Briefing Paper for Section 5 Inspectors*, Manchester: Ofsted.

Osler, A. (2010) *Students' Perspectives on Schooling*, Maidenhead: McGraw Hill.

Pearce, N. and Hillman, J. (1998) *Wasted Youth: Raising Achievement and Tackling Social Exclusion*, London: IPPR.

Pearson, S. (2010) 'The role of Special Educational Needs Co-ordinators: "To be or not to be"', *The Psychology of Education Review* 34 (2) pp30–38.

Peters, S. (2003) *Inclusive Education: Achieving Education for all by Including those with Disabilities and Special Educational Needs*, Geneva: World Bank.

Pettit, B. (2003) *Effective Joint Working between CAMHS and Schools, Research Report RR412*, London: DfES.

Pinkus, S. (2005) 'Bridging the gap between policy and practice: adopting a strategic vision for partnership working in special education', *British Journal of Special Education* 34(2) pp184–187.

Pring, R. (2000) *Philosophy of Educational Research*, London: Continuum.

Qualifications and Curriculum Authority (1999) *National Curriculum Inclusion Statement*, Norwich: HMSO.

Quicke, J. (1997) 'Reflexivity, community and education for the learning society', *Curriculum Studies* 5(2) pp139–162.

Rae, T. (2010) 'How to use nurture groups to promote inclusion in early years: emotional literacy and self confidence', *Social and Emotional Learning Update*, 23 September.

Rayner, S. (2007) *Managing Special and Inclusive Education*, London: Sage.

—— (2009) 'Educational Diversity and learning leadership: a proposition, some principles and a model of inclusive leadership', *Educational Review* 61(4) pp433–477.

Richards, G. (2010) 'I feel confident about teaching but SEN scares me. Moving from anxiety to confidence', in G. Richards and F. Armstrong *Teaching and Learning in Diverse and Inclusive Classrooms: Key Issues for New Teachers*, Abingdon: Routledge.

Richards, G. and Armstrong, F. (2010) *Teaching and Learning in Diverse and Inclusive Classrooms: Key Issues for New Teachers*, Abingdon: Routledge.

Richards, G., Anderson, A. and Drury, P. (2007) *Responding to Learners' Views*, London: Learning and Skills Development Agency.

Richmond, R. (1979) 'Warnock: found wanting and waiting', *Special Education – Forward Trends* 6(3) pp8–10.

Riddell, S. (2002) *Special Educational Needs* (Policy and Practice in Education series), Edinburgh: Dunedin Academic Press.

Riehl, C. (2000) 'The principal's role in creating inclusive schools for diverse students: a review of normative, empirical and critical literature on the practice of educational administration', *Review of Educational Research* 70(1) pp55–81.

Rieser, R. (2001) 'Does language matter?' *Inclusion Now* 2 pp16–17.

—— (2011) 'The schools white paper: progress or profiteering?' *Inclusion Now* 28 pp6–7.

Rieser, R. and Mason, M. (1992) *Disability Equality in the Classroom: A Human Rights Issue*, London: Disability Equality in Education.

Rioux, M. (2002) 'Disability, citizenship and rights in a changing world', in C. Barnes, M. Oliver and L. Barton (eds) *Disability Studies Today*, Cambridge: Polity.

Rix, J., Nind, M., Sheehy, K., Simmons, K. and Walsh, C. (eds) (2010) *Equality, Participation and Inclusion 1. Diverse Perspectives*, Abingdon: Routledge.

Roaf, C. (2002) *Co-ordinating Services for Including Children and Young People: Joined up Action*, Buckingham: Open University Press.

Roaf, C. and Bines, H. (eds) (1989) *Needs, Rights and Opportunities*, London: Falmer.

—— (2004) 'Needs, rights and opportunities', in G. Thomas and M. Vaughan (eds) *Inclusive Education: Readings and Reflections*, Maidenhead: Open University Press.

Robinson, K. (2011 [2001]) *Out of Our Minds: Learning to be Creative*, Chichester: Capstone.

Rose, J. and Bennathan, M. (2003) *Back on Track: A Strategy for Modernising Alternative Provision for Young People, Response of the Nurture Group Network*, London: Nurture Group Network.

Roulstone, A. and Prideaux, S. (2008) 'More policies, greater inclusion? Exploring the contradictions of New Labour inclusive education policy', *International Studies in Sociology of Education*, 18(1) pp15–29.

Runswick-Cole, K. and Hodge, N. (2009) 'Needs or rights? A challenge to the discourse of special education', *British Journal of Special Education* 36(4) pp198–203.

Rustemeier, S. (2002) *Social and Educational Justice: The Human Rights Framework for Inclusion*, Bristol: CSIE.

Ryan, J. (2006a) 'Inclusive leadership and social justice in schools', *Leadership and Policy in Schools* 5 pp3–17.

—— (2006b) *Inclusive Leadership*, San Francisco, CA: Jossey-Bass.

Salend, S., Johansen, M., Mumper, J., Chase, A., Pike, K. and Dorney, J. (1997) 'Co-operative teaching: the voices of two teachers', *Remedial and Special Education* 18(1) pp3–11.

Salt, T. (2010) The *Salt Review: Independent Review of Teacher Supply for Pupils with Severe, Profound and Multiple Learning Difficulties*, London: DSCF.

Save the Children, Norway (2008) *Lao PDR Diary*, Ventiane: Save the Children, Norway.

Sayed, Y. (1997) 'The concept of quality in education: a view from South Africa', in K. Watson, C. Modgil and S. Modgil (eds) *Educational Dilemmas: Debate and Diversity*, London: Cassell.

Shaeffer, S. (1999) *A Framework for Rights-based, Child-friendly Schools*. Available at: http://www.unicef.org/lifeskills/index_7260.html (accessed 27 March 2010).

Shepherd, J. (2009) 'Fertile minds need feeding', The *Guardian*, 10 February.

Sherman, R. and Webb, R. (eds) (1988) *Qualitative Research in Education: Focus and Methods*, London: RoutledgeFalmer.

Sindelar, P., Shearer, D., Yendol-Hoppey, D. and Liebert, T. (2006) 'The sustainability of inclusive school reform', *Exceptional Children*, 72(3) pp317–331.

Siraj-Blatchford, I., Clarke, K. and Needham, M. (2007) *The Team Around the Child: Multi-agency Working in the Early Years*, Stoke-on-Trent: Trentham Books.

Slee, R. (1996) 'Clauses of conditionality: the "reasonable" accommodation of language', in L. Barton (ed.) *Disability and Society: Emerging Issues and Insights*, Essex: Longman.

—— (2001) 'Driven to the Margins: disabled students, inclusive schooling and the politics of possibility', *Cambridge Journal of Education* 31(3) pp385–397.

—— (2004) 'Inclusive education: a framework for school reform', in V. Heung and M. Ainscow (eds) *Inclusive Education: A Framework for Reform*, Hong Kong: Institute of Education.

—— (2006) 'Limits to and possibilities for educational reform', *International Journal of Inclusive Education* 10(2–3) pp109–119.

Slee, R., Weiner, G. and Tomlinson, S. (2005) *School Effectiveness for Whom? Challenges to the School Effectiveness and School Improvement Movements*, London: RoutledgeFalmer.

Sloper, P. (2004) 'Facilitators and barriers for co-ordinated multi-agency services', *Child: Care, Health and Development* 30(6) pp571–580.

Soan, S. (2004) *Additional Educational Needs: Inclusive Approaches to Teaching*, London: David Fulton.

—— (2006) 'Are the needs of children and young people with social, emotional and behavioural needs being served within a multi-agency framework?' *Support for Learning* 21(4) pp210–215.

Soan, S. with The Caldecott Foundation (2010) *Improving Outcomes for Looked-After Children: A Practical Guide to Raising Aspirations and Achievement*, London: Optimus Education.

Sockett, H. (1993) *The Moral Base for Teacher Professionalism*, New York: Teachers College Press.

—— (2006) (ed.) *Teacher Dispositions: Building a Teacher Education Framework of Moral Standards*, Washington, DC: American Association of Colleges for Teacher Education.

Söderström, S. and Ytterhus, B. (2010) 'The use and non-use of assistive technologies from the world of information and communication technology by visually impaired young people: a walk on the tightrope of peer inclusion', *Disability and Society* 25(3) pp303–315.

Song, H. (2010) 'Co-operative action research in a "learning in regular classrooms" school', in C. Forlin (ed.) *Teacher Education For Inclusion: Changing Paradigms and Innovative Approaches*, London: Routledge.

Sriprakash, A. (2010) 'Child-centred education and the promise of democratic learning: pedagogic messages in rural Indian primary schools', *International Journal of Educational Development* 30(3) pp297–304.

Stead, J., Lloyd, G. and Kendrick, A. (2004) 'Participation or practice innovation: tensions in inter-agency working to address disciplinary exclusion from school', *Children and Society* 18(1) pp42–52.

Stephens, D. (2007) *Culture in Education and Development*, Oxford: Symposium Books.

Stuart-Fox, M. (1997) *A History of Laos*, Cambridge: Cambridge University Press.

Svensson, C. and Middlemas, B. (2010) 'Assessment for effective practice', in F. Hallett and G. Hallet *Transforming the role of the SENCO*, Maidenhead: Open University Press.

Szwed, C. (2007a) 'Managing from the middle? Tensions and dilemmas in the role of the primary school special educational needs co-ordinator', *School Leadership and Management* 27(1) pp437–451.

—— (2007b) 'Reconsidering the role of the primary special educational needs co-ordinator: Policy, practice and future priorities', *British Journal of Special Education* 34(2) pp96–104.

Tassoni, P. (2003) *Signposting Special Needs: Understanding Inclusion in the Early Years*, Oxford: Heinemann.

Theocharis, G. and Couston-Theocharis, J. (2008) 'Oppressors or emancipators: critical dispositions for preparing inclusive school leaders', *Equity and Excellence in Education* 41(2) pp230–246.

Thomas, G. and Loxley, A. (2001) *Deconstructing Special Education and Constructing Inclusion*, Buckingham: Open University Press.

—— (2007) 'Inclusive schools in an inclusive society? Policy, politics and paradox', in G. Thomas and A. Loxley *Deconstructing Special Education and Constructing Inclusion*, Maidenhead: Open University Press.

Thomas, G. and Vaughan, M. (2004) *Inclusive Education: Readings and Reflections*, Maidenhead: Open University Press.

Thomas, G., Walker, D. and Webb, J. (1998) *The Making of the Inclusive School*, London: Routledge.

Tilstone, C., Florian, L. and Rose, R. (eds) (2002) *Promoting Inclusive Practice*, London: Routledge.

Tomlinson, S. (1982) *A Sociology of Special Education*, London: Routledge and Kegan Paul.

Training and Development Agency for Schools (2009) Specification for nationally approved traning from SENCOs. Available at: http://www.tda.gov.uk/~/media/resources/teacher/sen/national_senco_training_specification.pdf?keywords=SENCo+Training (accessed 9 September 2011).

Trompenaars, F. and Hampden-Turner, C. (1997) *Riding the Waves of Culture*, London: Nicholas Brealey.

Underwood, J. and Underwood, G. (1990) *Computers and Learning: Helping Children Acquire Thinking Skills*, Oxford: Blackwell.

UNESCO (1994) The Salamanca Statement and Framework for Action on Special Needs Education, adopted by the World Conference on Special Needs Education: Access and Quality, Salamanca, Spain, 7–10 June 1994.

—— (2005) *Guidelines for Inclusion: Ensuring Access to Education for All*, Paris: UNESCO.

—— (2008) 'Education for all by 2015: will we make it? Summary', *Global Monitoring Report*, Paris: UNESCO.

—— (2009) *Embracing Diversity: Toolkit for Creating Inclusive Learning-Friendly Environments*, UNESCO: Asia-Pacific Programme of Education for All.

UNICEF (2007) *Child Poverty in Perspective: An Overview of Child Well-Being in Rich Countries*, Report Card 7, Florence: UNICEF Innocenti Research Centre.

United Nations (1982) *United Nations World Programme of Action Concerning Disabled Persons*, New York: UN.

—— (1989) *Convention on the Rights of the Child*, New York: UN.

—— (2008) *Education for All by 2015: Will we make it?* Paris: UNESCO.

Vygotsky, L. (1987) *Thought and Language: Revised Edition*, Cambridge, MA: MIT Press.

Wagner, P. (1994) *A Sociology of Modernity: Liberty and Discipline*, London/New York: Routledge.

Warmington, P., Daniels, H., Edwards, A., Brown, S., Leadbetter, J., Martin, D. and Middleton, D. (2004) *TLRPIII: Learning in and for Inter-agency Working. Inter-agency Collaboration: A Review of the Literature*, Birmingham: University of Birmingham.

Warnock, M. (2005) *Special Educational Needs: A New Look*, London: Philosophy of Education Society of Great Britain.

Wearmouth, J. (2009) *A Beginning Teacher's Guide to Special Educational Needs*, Maidenhead: Open University Press.

Wedell, K. (2009) 'SENCO-FORUM: points from the SENCO-forum: recent legislation and SENCOs' work', *British Journal of Special Education* 36(3) p174.

Wenger, E. (1998) *Communities of Practice: Learning, Meaning, and Identity*, Cambridge: Cambridge University Press.

Wing, L. (1996) *The Autistic Spectrum*, London: Constable.

Woods, P., Jeffrey, B., Tronman, G. and Boyle, M. (1997) *Restructuring Schools, Restructuring Teachers: Responding to Change in the Primary School*, Buckingham: Open University Press.

World Bank (2008) *The Road to 2015: Reaching the Education Goals, Education for All Fast Track Initiative*, Washington, DC: World Bank.

Wrigley, T. (2011) 'Editorial', *Improving Schools* 14(1) pp3–4.

Zigmoid, N. and Baker, J. (1996) 'Full inclusion for students with learning disabilities: too much of a good thing', *Theory into Practice* 35(1) pp26–34.

Index

Bold page numbers indicate figures, italics indicate tables.